DIVISION STREET

A Comedy

by

STEVE TESICH

SAMUEL FRENCH, INC.

25 WEST 45TH STREET   NEW YORK 10036
7623 SUNSET BOULEVARD   HOLLYWOOD 90046
LONDON   *TORONTO*

31444

CAST

(in order of appearance)

Chris .... JOHN LITHGOW

Mrs. Bruchinski .... THERESA MERRITT

Yovan .... KEENE CURTIS

Betty .... JUSTIN LORD

Nadja .... MURPHY CROSS

Roger .... JOE REGALBUTO

Dianah .... CHRISTINE LAHTI

Sal .... ANTHONY HOLLAND

TIME: The Present

PLACE: Chicago

TEMPO: Allegro con Sentimento

THERE WILL BE ONE INTERMISSION

UNDERSTUDIES

Understudies never substitute for listed players unless a specific announcement
for the appearance is made at the time of the performance.

For Chris—Raymond Baker; for Mrs. Bruchinski—Barbara Meek; for Betty—Stephen
Burks; for Yovan—George Touliatos; for Roger & Sal—Stephen Van Benschoten; for Dianah
and Nadja—Joy Rinaldi.

THE SET

MRS. BRUCHINSKI'S HOUSE
(The entrance to the house is Stage Right. A stairway leads to CHRIS ADRIAN'S *apartment. Opposite the entrance to his apartment is* MRS. BRUCHINSKI'S *apartment. All we see of it is her door. Both her door and* CHRIS'S *door open out. When both doors are opened they just about touch.*

CHRIS' APARTMENT
The apartment is essentially one room. There is a window looking out on the street. A bedroom: all we see is the door. The same is true of the bathroom. There is a kitchen area, a sofa, and boxes containing what's left of CHRIS'S *life. The room has been furnished by* MRS. BRUCHINSKI.

THE STREET
. . . Surrounds the apartment and is connected organically to the building. It contains a couple of benches, a playphone and perhaps an interesting street sign with the words: DIVISION STREET.

DIVISION STREET

ACT I

Lights come up on CHRIS' *apartment. He is asleep on the sofa totally covered by a quilt. The alarm clock rings. He leaps out of bed, rushes to shut it off. Opens the window and yells.*

CHRIS. Hey, you! Paper boy! (*A paper shoots through the window just missing him*) I told you yesterday, I don't have a subscription, damn it. (*He tries to shut the window. He can't*) Oh no! Not again! (CHRIS *tries real hard to shut the window. It won't close*) MRS. BRUCHINSKI! (*Pause*) MRS. BRUCHINSKI!

MRS. BRUCHINSKI. (*Offstage*) YES, VAT IS IT?

CHRIS. COULD YOU PLEASE COME HERE? (*He sits on the window ledge*)

MRS. BRUCHINSKI. YES, I COULD.

CHRIS. ARE YOU COMING?

MRS. BRUCHINSKI. ARE YOU VAITING?

CHRIS. YES, I AM.

MRS. BRUCHINSKI. I AM COMING.

(MRS. BRUCHINSKI *walks out of her apartment, through the landing, and into* CHRIS' *apartment. She is Black and speaks with a Polish accent.* SHE *carries a newspaper.*)

I am here. So vat is big dill.

CHRIS. I don't feel well, and the garbage I smell is

7

upsetting the garbage I ate last night. The window is stuck open again!

Mrs. Bruchinski. SHTUCK! DID YOU SAY SHTUCK?

(*She slams the door shut and as She does the window comes down.* Chris *just looks on wondering what to do next.*)

Not to worry. I'm Polish. I fix it nothing flat.

(*But she is rolling up her sleeves and coming toward him.* Chris *is desperate. He doesn't want her to open the window.*)

Chris. You fixed it already. It's closed. I like it closed.
Mrs. Bruchinski. It's shtuck closed. I hate shtuck. I make it unshtuck.

(*She pushes* Chris *out of the way. Speaks to the window.*)

Okay, vindow. I make you sorry you ever shtuck you somonabitch. (*She lunges at it and tries to open it. She laughs*) It's shtuck all right. (*She tries it again.* Mrs. Bruchinski *is upset*) You somonabitch shtuck vindow, I fix your goose.

(*She tries to open it again. She grunts and groans.* Chris *gives up and walks away.* Mrs. Bruchinski *opens the window. She is delighted.*)

BRAVO FOR ME!
Chris. I have a terrible headache.
Mrs. Bruchinski. I saw your picture in the Polish Gazette. It is not very cute picture of you, Chris.

CHRIS. It's hard to look cute, Mrs. Bruchinski, when you're throwing up on the streets of Chicago.

MRS. BRUCHINSKI. You get drunk like skunk, no?

CHRIS. No. I don't drink. I shouldn't eat even. I went to this restaurant. New World Bar and Grill and I ordered the specialty of the house: Stuffed Cabbage a la Serbia.

MRS. BRUCHINSKI. I make very nice stuffed cabbage.

CHRIS. Maybe *you* do. The stuff I had made me sick to my stomach. I ran out in the street and as I was . . . throwing up . . . this photographer recognized me and started taking pictures of me. A.P. and U.P.I. picked it up and now my whole past is splattered on the front page of every newspaper in the country.

MRS. BRUCHINSKI. Yes, I know. I did not know I had such famous big shot radical leader living in my house.

CHRIS. That was during the 60's Mrs. Bruchinski. I don't do that radical stuff anymore. There are no radicals left anywhere. The last few I heard about were into Coors beer and solar power.

MRS. BRUCHINSKI. That I don't know. You come to Chicago to make revolution?

CHRIS. Oh. c'mon. Do I look like a revolutionary?

MRS. BRUCHINSKI. Do I look Polish. There you go. You come to town to make Power to the People.

CHRIS. No. Absolutely, positively no.

MRS. BRUCHINSKI. Why not?

CHRIS. Because I don't want to do that stuff anymore.

MRS. BRUCHINSKI. Too bad. I was hoping to make some kind revolution. Nothing fancy. But nice. You know.

CHRIS. Oh give me a break, Mrs. Bruchinski.

MRS. BRUCHINSKI. We have such fine country, Chris, and it makes me sick nobody gives not one damn anymore. By damn, it is time to give one damn again. Time to march on Washington again and make dream come true.

CHRIS. I came to Chicago with only one dream, Mrs. Bruchinski. To get a job. I don't give a damn about anything else.

MRS. BRUCHINSKI. For shame.

CHRIS. That's how it is. I want to punch the clock and work on my seniority so that I can have a nice pension when the time comes.

MRS. BRUCHINSKI. You don't make march on Washington?

CHRIS. No.

MRS. BRUCHINSKI. Maybe you change your mind?

CHRIS. Mrs. Bruchinski . . . please. I want this job and if I'm going to get it I have to write something very, very important. I need peace and quiet all weekend.

MRS. BRUCHINSKI. It is too peace and quiet for me, Chris.

CHRIS. Mrs. Bruchinski I need your help. You see, the old man Kellogg who lived here before me . . .

MRS. BRUCHINSKI. He's dead. Shtuck in the grave. (*She laughs at her own joke*) You don't hear such good jokes on TV. Boy, oh boy.

CHRIS. Yes, I know he's dead but his habits live on. He had some weird arrangement with the paper boy. If I don't open the window on the dot the paper goes right through the glass. I've replaced two panes already. And then there's the milk. Somebody keeps delivering milk. And then there's the pimp. Do you know what a pimp is Mrs. Bruchinski?

MRS. BRUCHINSKI. Pimp? I should hope not. But despite everything I still know. I know pimp. I know Spanish fly. I know French tickler. I don't vant to know. But I know. You know what I mean.

CHRIS. This pimp Arnold keeps calling me, Mrs. Bruchinski. He thinks I'm old man Kellogg. I've gathered from our conversations that I've been paid up for a year's worth of whores. One a month. He wants to know which one I want.

MRS. BRUCHINSKI. The Japanese one is nice. If you got yen for Japanese. (*She laughs at her joke*) Yen for Japanese. Get it.

CHRIS. Mrs. Bruchinski, please. You see I think the crazy old man Kellogg . . .

MRS. BRUCHINSKI. STOP! Old man Kellogg not crazy. He was fine old man. He paid everything year ahead of time. Rent, newspapers, milk, whores. Everything. (*She gets a little sentimental. Tear in her eye*) Old man and I . . . we did hanky and panky during whore's strike. I even had small baby boy. Old man was not so old then, but he was very forgetful. He took small baby son out for walk and forgot where he left him. I was very angry vith him. I raise his rent. That's last thing I raise for the old man. (*Laughs at joke*) Now I am all alone. Old woman. All alone. Where is my little baby boy? Ah, Chris, there was a better time for me. I once did "We Shall Overcome." In Washington, District of Columbia. It was so beautiful. So many people . . . marching and singing . . . like big family. And a voice from a man I could not see — saying "I have a dream."

(*She begins to sing "We Shall Overcome" and exits slowly.* CHRIS *feels something as she sings. It is not something he wants to feel. When she exits he tries to shut the window by slamming the door shut. It doesn't work. He picks up the newspaper. His actions are ones of a person ready to tear the newspaper to shreds who controls himself. He throws it out of the window. He tries to close the window. He can't. The door opens.* YOVAN, *dark, handsome, dressed like a Mafia tailor, enters. He is carrying a container with several quarts of milk in one hand and newspapers in the other. He looks at* CHRIS. CHRIS *is jumping up and down putting weight on the window, trying to close it.*)

YOVAN. Allo there.

(CHRIS *turns around.* YOVAN *slams the door shut. The window goes down.*)

YOVAN. Your milk is getting warm, Mr. Disgusting.
CHRIS. Who're you?
YOVAN. My name is Yovan. I come from the old country an I have a snit to pick with you.
CHRIS. Are you the milk man?
YOVAN. I am man for all seasons. Put milk in fridge.
CHRIS. It's not my milk and my fridge is full of milk as it is. Who the hell . . .

(YOVAN *pulls gun on* CHRIS.)

YOVAN. PUT MILK IN FRIDGE BEFORE MILK SPOIL . . . YOU . . . YOU . . . ROTTEN CONSUMER YOU!

(YOVAN *throws the milk carrier on the ottoman. The gun frightens* CHRIS.)

CHRIS. Sure. Why not. Yes. Milk in fridge.
YOVAN. Little babies in Peru cry out from hunger in the night and you let milk spoil. You . . . you . . . rotten human being.

(*The gun is still on* CHRIS. *He takes the milk carefully and starts for the fridge.* HE *has made a big show of putting milk in fridge. There's a lot of milk there already.*)

CHRIS. (*Slams door of fridge closed*) There. Milk in fridge.

YOVAN. COME HERE!

(CHRIS *comes Down to the sofa, arms up, and sits. His stomach and head are acting up again.*)

YOVAN. You have seen the newspapers, no?

CHRIS. Yes.

YOVAN. Look at pictures in papers . . . You recognize your ugly self?

(CHRIS *looks at them.*)

CHRIS. Sure do. It's my ugly self all right.

YOVAN. Look at picture one more time again. You see the name of restaurant behind your puking face?

CHRIS. I know the name of restaurant. It's New World Bar and Grill. Barf and Grill is more like it.

(CHRIS *laughs trying to humor* YOVAN. YOVAN *is like a stone wall.*)

YOVAN. You are so hilarious it is going to murder you. I am proud owner of New World Bar and Grill.

(CHRIS, *despite his fear of the gun, is a little angry now.*)

CHRIS. You should fire your chef, man. He almost killed me.

YOVAN. I am chef, sucker man . . .

CHRIS. Well, Mr. Stuffed Cabbage . . . Do you know what you have done. You've ruined everything. Nobody knew I was in Chicago. Now my wife Dianah knows. Who knows who else knows. And those that knew me in Chicago didn't know who I was. Now they know all about me.

YOVAN. Excellent. I hope your life is in ruins.

CHRIS. My job is, thanks to you. I was supposed to start work today. But oh no . . . My boss saw that picture and read that story about me and now if I want to work for him I have to write a retraction of my Radical Past for the Chicago Sun-Times, write it quickly, and write it so he likes it . . . and it's all your fault.

YOVAN. STOP!

(*He sticks the gun into* CHRIS' *stomach.* CHRIS *gets quiet. All is quiet.*)

You have just screamed at me. Now I am going to make scream at you. Do you know what you have done. You bring bad publicity on me. Your picture in all the papers of Chicago.

(*Goes through the papers, flinging them at* CHRIS.)

Polish Sun. Polish Tribune. Lithuanian Gazette. Croatian Times. Polish Times. Polish Gazette. You make me laughing stock of Chicago nationalities! He, he, he, they all go at me. Ha, ha, ha. I got telephone calls in various languages and they all go: Ho, Ho, Ho.

CHRIS. Sounds like a lot of laughs.

YOVAN. Don't get humorous with me! Your blood, Mr. Rotten Manners, will wash away the insult if you do not make sorry. Make sorry. And make it good and quick. I am not talking chupped liver . . . Mr. Redical of the Sixties. I am talking proper apple-logy.

CHRIS. Apple-logy! You want *me* to apologize. To *you*. After what *you've* done to *me* . . . Well, I'm not going to apologize. I don't apologize. You have your pride. I have my pride.

YOVAN. I also have a gun.

(*He fires the gun in the air and then aims it at* CHRIS. MRS. BRUCHINSKI *runs in. She sees* YOVAN *with the gun.*)

MRS. BRUCHINSKI. Sorry. Did not know you had company, Kris. Bye-bye.

(*She goes out again. The firing of the gun has made* CHRIS *settle down a bit.* YOVAN *looks at the door.*)

YOVAN. Funny accent for black lady. Anyways, getting back to brass tacks. Here is offer. You come back to my restaurant.

CHRIS. Never.

YOVAN. Monday. You come back and you sit down at nice table and you eat my food. And you look happy when you eat. You go: Mmmm, yummy, yummy, yummy. In the middle of yumm I take snapshot of you with my Polaroid Pronto. I send picture to all the papers and you write apple-logy with John Hancock on the bottom.

CHRIS. You think I'm crazy.

YOVAN. No. I think I am crazy. I am crazy with anger. I make cement hushpuppies for your feet. Get it.

CHRIS. Hey, give me a break, buddy.

YOVAN. DO NOT GET FAMILIAR. We did not pick walnuts together in our youth.

CHRIS. Look let's be reasonable, all right?

YOVAN. Okee-dokey.

CHRIS. We've done enough harm to each other already. I've ruined your reputation. You've got me in trouble with my boss, with my wife . . .

YOVAN. At least you have wife.

CHRIS. I don't want wife.

YOVAN. I want wife. My wife, the cook, she died. She left no recipes behind.

(*He is getting sentimental. He might even drape his arm around* CHRIS.)

I miss my wife.

CHRIS. I bet all your customers do, too.

YOVAN. Yes, is true. Poof, she died. Then my daughter Nadja, poof . . .

CHRIS. She died?

YOVAN. No such luck. She run off with some man, Roger, whose hide and hair I never even see. The son I never had I still don't have. A big family is what I always wanted, like Italians and Puerto Ricans and what do I have. Big loneliness is what I have. (*Tears come to his eyes*) Alone I sit on my waterbed like ship-wrecked sailor far far from shore of mother country. (*He is weeping. Starts to sing*) Tamo, daleko . . . Daleko kraj mora. Tamo je moja Mama . . . Tamo je Srbija . . . (*He can't sing. Tears choke him. He sobs*) Ah, Redical of the Sixties. I am so unhappy. I love America but America does not love me.

CHRIS. Sure she does.

YOVAN. No, no, no. There was time . . . Yes. No more. Is every man for himself now.

CHRIS. (*Interrupting*) Well, you've certainly had a rough time of it. I can't say it's been exactly easy for me either. I guess we just have to be flexible . . . and . . . well, forget the past.

YOVAN. Forget! I forget nothing. Such psychology roll off me like water off the ass of duck.

CHRIS. In that case I suggest you put the ass of duck on your menu. I have already agreed to apologize for having been alive just to keep my job, and I'll be damned if I'll now apologize for having almost died.

YOVAN. Okee-dokey. I fix your goose, you turkey. Your cork has popped. Your bottle of wine is breathing its last. The telephone is ringing in the house of the man who will be digging your grave. (YOVAN *opens the window and starts going out*)

CHRIS. What the hell you doing now?

YOVAN. Old tradition. We never cross threshold twice of man we threaten to kill. And remember this, Mr. Smartie Panties: sometimes, somehow, somewhere when you least expect it . . . it is not going to be Allen Funt of Candid Camera. Get it!

(CHRIS *picks up the papers.* YOVAN *vanishes through the window.*)

CHRIS. You just don't shoot people for having an upset stomach. (CHRIS *throws papers out of the window. He is trying to get a hold of himself. There's not much there.* CHRIS *looks out window*) Hey, you, get away from my car, dammit.

(*A shot is heard.*)

He shot my car! I don't believe this. He shot my car.

(*Another shot — the window slams shut.*)

He shot it again. That's it! That does it. You can't shoot my T-Bird and get away with it. (*He staggers to the telephone. Dials*) Hello, Operator, get me the Police! Hello, Police! This Alien from the New World Bar and Grill where I barfed is threatening to kill me if I don't go "yummy, yummy" and make an apple-logy. And now he just shot my bird. Hello! Hello!

(*He hangs up.* MRS. BRUCHINSKI *enters.*)

MRS. BRUCHINSKI. Killer man gone?
CHRIS. Yes. He just shot my car.

(*She slams door. Crosses to window.*)

MRS. BRUCHINSKI. Sonomogun window shtuck closed again.
CHRIS. (*Goes into bedroom*) I'm going down to the police station and scream at the cops.

(MRS. BRUCHINSKI *trying to open window. Just as she opens the window the door opens and* BETTY, *the Black cop, who was once a male, enters. She's carrying an armful of newspapers.*)

BETTY. All right, sister. Cool it. I got a complaint from people across the street about a litterbug throwing newspapers out of the window.

(CHRIS *comes out of the bedroom.* BETTY *sees* CHRIS *and throws the papers down.*)

CHRIS. Police! God, that was quick.
BETTY. CHRIS! CHRISTOPHER MY MAN! CHRIS BABY!

(SHE *primps a little, wanting to look good for* CHRIS.)

CHRIS. Who the hell are you?

BETTY. Damn. Been so long. Remember J.B. Kellogg?

CHRIS. No.

BETTY. Remember? Bomber Kellogg.

CHRIS. No.

BETTY. You do so.

CHRIS. So what? All right, I do.

BETTY. It's me! J.B.!

CHRIS. J.B. was a man.

BETTY. I was a man.

MRS. BRUCHINSKI. Somonabitch!

BETTY. I got myself a sex change a while ago and . . .

CHRIS. I don't believe any of this.

BETTY. Oh, Chrissie. It's like old times. Give me five!

CHRIS. Give me a break.

(CHRIS *makes it out of the window as* BETTY *comes toward him.* BETTY *shouts after him.*)

BETTY. Where the hell you going?

MRS. BRUCHINSKI. Kris is going to make scrims at cops in police station.

BETTY. Give 'em hell, Chris.

(BETTY *does a long look at* MRS. BRUCHINSKI.)

Hey, Mama, you sure do look like a soul sister but you sure don't sound like no soul sister.

MRS. BRUCHINSKI. You too. You look like soul sister but you make sounds like soul brother. You were a man once.

BETTY. Sister, I was many things once. Chris and I and Roger O'Dwyer and Stokely and Rennie Davis . . . We were going to change the world, sister.

MRS. BRUCHINSKI. So was I. Such songs we used to sing marching together in the streets of Washington.

BETTY. I marched in Washington when Martin was there. I was just a boy.

MRS. BRUCHINSKI. You were a boy?

BETTY. At one time.

MRS. BRUCHINSKI. I was a mama. At one time.

BETTY. I had a mama. At one time.

(*They look at each other. There is something in the air for a split second and then they shoo it away with their hands.*)

MRS. BRUCHINSKI. Now it is all gone. Cute baby boy gone. Rotten old man gone. We shall overcome . . . gone. When will "Overcome" come again?

(*She starts to sing: "We Shall Overcome." She of course weeps when she sings.* BETTY *joins in and* BETTY *weeps a little too. They sing as they exit.* BETTY *slams the door shut. The window goes down again.* MRS. BRUCHINSKI *goes into her apartment.* BETTY *goes down the stairs and into the street, singing or humming.* NADJA, *the slut, is coming onto the street. She stops to peddle. Hitchhike.*)

BETTY. Hey, don't strut that trashy stuff around here, you hear.

(NADJA *turns around.*)

NADJA. Look . . . Hi there, Betty.

BETTY. Hey, Nadja. How's business?

NADJA. I got a new pimp Arnold, and Arnold's got me a gig with this old man Chris. He's paid up for the year. It could mean a steady job.

BETTY. Just saw my man Chris, a former comrade from the days of the barricades. You're too young to know, Nadja, but those were the days. I was a man then and . . . well . . . the times we lived in had balls . . . and I had them too . . . and now . . .

NADJA. I think you look wonderful, Betty. That's the best transsexual operation I've ever seen.

BETTY. Well, thank you, Nadja. Coming from a fellow sister that's quite a compliment.

NADJA. They're going to let you stay on the force?

BETTY. DAMN right. They tried kicking me off but according to the Fed guidelines they have to hire so many minority transsexuals. Girl, I just love your perfume.

(NADJA *takes perfume. Sprays* BETTY.)

NADJA. It's called "Revenge." It used to drive my husband Roger crazy.

BETTY. Crazy! I like it.

NADJA. Got to go, Betty, Catch you later.

(*They kiss.*)

I guess your beard's still a problem.

BETTY. That's the least of my problems, Nadja.

NADJA. Bye, Bye.

BETTY. Bye.

(NADJA *strolls Off.* BETTY *takes out a battery-operated shaver and shaves her face. Enter* ROGER. *He is an old man dressed in rags. He is carrying a bunch of newspapers under one arm. He has 2 bags in the other arm. Slung around his neck is his "box" — a radio-cassette machine. On the cassette, we hear: "Those Were The Days." He is walking toward* BETTY, *who is shaving. He is the saddest looking person in the world. As he comes near* BETTY, *he sniffs the air.)*

ROGER. NADJA!
BETTY. The name's Betty, Gramps!
ROGER. That perfume!
BETTY. It's called Revenge.
ROGER. I know it's Revenge. My wife Nadja used to wear it.

(He looks at BETTY. HE *walks toward the entrance to* CHRIS'S *building.* BETTY *strolls away. She is thinking about something.* ROGER *is thinking about something, too. Both turn around at the same time and look at each other.)*

ROGER. Weren't you . . .

(Both decide they were wrong about something, or maybe wrong. No, it couldn't be who each of them thought it was. BETTY *strolls Off as* ROGER *walks up the stairs toward* CHRIS *apartment.* MRS. BRUCHINSKI *opens the door. Sees* ROGER. *Hears music. Starts to sing.* ROGER, *stunned, joins her. They sing for a bit.* ROGER *breaks into tears and shuts off the cassett.)*

MRS. BRUCHINSKI. Who are you old man and vat is it you vant with me in this terrible don't give a damn times we live in.

ROGER. I want to fall through a time warp. I want to make up for ten wasted years. I want meaning in my life again.

MRS. BRUCHINSKI. Me too old man poopsy. You want revolution maybe.

ROGER. Maybe later.

MRS. BRUCHINSKI. You want cup of tea, maybe now.

ROGER. Now, I just want Chris in my life again.

MRS. BRUCHINSKI. Kris is not home. He went out to scrim at the police.

ROGER. He would! The old rebel! He's still at it.

MRS. BRUCHINSKI. My name is Mrs. Bruchinski.

ROGER. My name is Roger. Roger the Rotten. Roger the Rebel no more.

MRS. BRUCHINSKI. Please to meet you old man poopsy.

(ROGER *starts going into* CHRIS *place.*)

MRS. BRUCHINSKI. Nice to have old man again. Brings back memories of hanky and panky.

ROGER. Forgive me, Chris!

(*Sirens wail as* DIANAH *and* SAL *enter.* DIANAH *is carrying a bullhorn and a newspaper.* SAL *a briefcase.*)

DIANAH. Chris!

ROGER. CHRIS!

DIANAH. OH CHRIS!

ROGER. Oh, Chris, oh, Chris!

(ROGER *sinks back on the floor.* DIANAH *weeps.*)

DIANAH. Chris! Chris! Chris!

SAL. Here we are. This is his address.

DIANAH. This is terrible. Chris Adrian. My husband. Throwing his life away.

SAL. He's throwing more than his life according to that picture.

DIANAH. Hush . . . you . . . You . . . lawyer.

SAL. I may be a lawyer but I'm also a man. You may still be his wife but you're also a woman.

DIANAH. A job. He told me on the telephone that he got a job. A full time middle class job. Oh, Chicago, Chicago, you toddling town, blow my tears away.

SAL. I'll kiss your tears away if you let me.

DIANAH. This isn't the Chris I know. I bet he's been brainwashed. He needs to be de-programmed. I need legal advice. I'll have to get a lawyer.

SAL. I am a lawyer. Remember me. You got me from legal aid. I'm talking to you, Dianah. Can you hear me?

DIANAH. At least I'm here. Close to him.

SAL. You're wasting your time, Dianah.

DIANAH. Let the time go by. I don't really care if I'm . . . on the street where he lives.

SAL. He left you. He didn't even tell you where he was going. A woman like you.

DIANAH. The way his smile just beams. The way he sings off key. The way he haunts my dream. No, no, they can't take that away from me.

SAL. But, Dianah, he's a bastard. A bum. A puking, no good, sonovabitch. I'm talking to you, Dianah. Can you hear me? Is there something the matter with my voice that you can't hear me?

DIANAH. What a voice he had. He had and he was the voice of his time.

SAL. I am the voice of my time, Dianah. Is it my fault that the times are what they are?

(*She doesn't hear him.*)

DIANAH. We met in Chicago. The windy city blew us together. You could say it was Destiny.

SAL. I'll say whatever you want . . . Can you hear me, Dianah? You make me feel very insecure.

DIANAH. And in that troubled and turbulent time I trembled when I saw him on that glorious day in May . . . only yesterday when the world was young. There he was . . . in a crowd . . . and yet alone . . . with a bullhorn in his hand. He stood there like a cross between Che Guevara and Chuck Mangione. And when he put the bullhorn to his lips to speak . . . he didn't speak . . . he played. A born bullhorn player and he seemed to be playing only for me. HO-HO-HO-CHI-MINH! (*She almost sobs*) I didn't know Ho Chi Minh from Pinnochio at that time, but something in me stirred when I heard his voice. He cared. He cared a lot. He exuded an aroma of Cuban cigars and mimeo ink and his loose fitting army surplus garb could not hide the body of a tango dancer. A woman can tell such things. I swooned. He smiled. I swayed. He played. I died. Oh what a man he was. What a voice he had. An assertive voice without being overbearing. It was the voice of a man who enjoys hearing children laugh.

SAL. I love hearing children laugh. I never laughed as a child. I always meant to but something always came up.

DIANAH. What happened to him? Was it something I did that was his undoing or something I didn't do that did him in? I don't know. All I know is that I feel responsible. I let his spark die . . . The flame of the rebel became a charcoal lighter on the Bar-B-Que Pit of History.

(*She falls silent. This is* SAL'S *chance to speak. He jumps at it.*)

SAL. Look at me, Dianah. I'm right here. I'm easy to see. Look at me, please.

(*She looks but not really at him, through him and beyond.*)

You are looking at a desperate, homeless, friendless creature, Dianah. I just can't seem to make an impression on anyone. Even my parents. I was conceived on a Castro convertible at their friend's house. They never had sex at home. When I was a baby they'd leave me at home with a baby sitter and go and have sex in a motel, or in a hotel, or at a friend's house. They had friends everywhere and they never introduced me to any of them. One day they just didn't come back. They just forgot about me. I was raised by a baby sitter, Dianah, who charged six seventy-five an hour. My old man, Kellogg, that rotten old man of mine, paid her seven years in advance. But when the money ran out she left. I got a job to try and keep her, but I got laid off. I was ten. Out of a job at ten! The older I grew, the more I craved love and friends, the less the world seemed to care. I am nobody's memory. Nobody gets together on a rainy day and wonders: How's Sal Kellogg doing? What's Sal Kellogg up to? Pigeons starving to death will not eat my bread crumbs in the park. Dogs facing certain death in a dog pound will not go home with me. I send letters and checks to the starving of Guatemala but they don't write back. Scientology doesn't want me. Moonies don't want me. I could be had for a song but the world stops humming when Sal goes by. I would become a flasher but who would look. I talk to myself and even I don't listen. Are you listening, Dianah? (*He cries, kneeling to* DIANAH, *sobbing*) This is the single longest uninterrupted speech I have ever made, Dianah, and I hope it moved you.

(DIANAH *looks at him.*)

DIANAH. What were you saying?

(SAL *is desperate. He wants to make an impression on her. He flings himself at her making an amorous attempt.*)

SAL. I love you, Dianah. That's what I'm saying. I love you. Love. Love. Love.

(*She doesn't move.*)

(SAL *Screams. Falls on floor.*)

Oh, God.
    DIANAH. I think my guilt over what I've allowed to happen to Chris has made me frigid.
    SAL. Alaska is frigid too! But underneath your frozen tundra there is oil waiting to flow.
    DIANAH. I don't think you have the pipeline for the job, Sal.
    SAL. Hurt me! I don't care!

(*She clutches the bullhorn to her bosom.* CHRIS *enters, carrying what's left of his car — his car top. He looks very upset. He sees* DIANAH *just as she sees him.*)

DIANAH. Chris! Darling!
CHRIS. Dianah! Dammit!

(SAL *tries to make an impression on* CHRIS.)

SAL. Hello, my name is Sal Kellogg. I've been retained by Dianah Adrian in the matter of Adrian vs. Adrian.

(*Neither of them seems to hear him.*)

DIANAH. Here we are again, Chris. In the windy city. Only now the crowd is gone and it's just the two of us.

SAL. There's three of us here. Just for the record.

DIANAH. Ah, Chris, the way we were. If we had the chance to do it all again . . . would we . . . could we . . . memories . . . light the corners of my mind.

CHRIS. I think your mind's gone, Dianah. It's over. It's all over.

DIANAH. Why, Chris, why?

CHRIS. Because, Dianah, because.

DIANAH. Was it the women's movement? Did I steal the torch from your hand . . . and you couldn't live with yourself?

CHRIS. I can live with myself. I can't live with you.

SAL. You can't talk to her like this. You hear me?

(CHRIS *doesn't.*)

CHRIS. Dianah, please. I've had a rough day, so don't make it any rougher. The street sharks stripped my Bird. I've never seen anything like it. They had blow torches and jacks and yankers and pullers. They even had a foreman in charge of the operation. All I could salvage from my whole car was this.

DIANAH. A car! We don't have cars. We don't believe in cars!

CHRIS. We're not we, Dianah. We were we for too long. And while we were we, you were you, but I wasn't me. And I want to be me. I gotta be me . . . Now you got me talking in that way of yours. I'm sick and tired of it all, Dianah. I have O.D.'s on all those causes and issues. I don't care about the boat people, Dianah.

(DIANAH *lets out a scream of anguish.*)

I don't. I don't want to hear about another boat person again. I don't care about nuclear waste. To hell with it. I don't care about oil spills, third world dictators, wilderness preserves, or bilingual education. Sugar in kid's cereals. Don't care! I don't give a good goddamn about the ozone layer, the whales, the porpoises . . . the cute little baby seals . . . I don't know who's running Cambodia and I don't care! I don't even care if the Beatles ever get back together again. Anything that I have ever cared about. Anything that you have ever cared about, anything that anyone has ever cared about, I don't care about and I don't care that I don't care.

DIANAH. (*Quietly*) I understand.

CHRIS. No, you don't. If you understood you wouldn't say "I understand" like that. Don't you understand. I am tired of drinking black coffee out of earthen mugs that you made yourself. I want a cup and saucer and I want sugar in it. I don't care if I never see another mimeo machine or another cruddy leaflet again. Me. That's all I care about. Me. Me. Me. Wonderful, yummy, delicious me! I want a nice condominium without a stitch of macrame in it. I want a TV. A stereo. A toaster oven. Shag rugs. Designer towels. A big fridge. A huge fridge. I want a walk-in fridge. When do I want it? I WANT IT NOW.

DIANAH. Oh, my God, he's gone mad. Chris. Don't do this to yourself.

CHRIS. That's right Dianah, I'm starting a new life.

DIANAH. He's delirious.

CHRIS. I'm going to be an underwriter in an insurance company.

(DIANAH *screams.* CHRIS *starts to leave.*)

DIANAH. CHRIS! What about me?

(CHRIS *stops.*)

CHRIS. Frankly, Dianah, I don't give a damn. (*Optional* — CHRIS *runs Off with car top and exits.*)
DIANAH. Oh, my God. Chris! I think it's too late for legal aid. I'll have to get him a psychiatrist.
SAL. He's gone over the edge, Dianah. Anybody that walks around the city with a car top in his arms has made the big plunge. They're playing his song Dianah, and it's looney tunes, you hear me?
DIANAH. I am all alone now.
SAL. You have me.
DIANAH. I can't live alone. I'll throw myself in Lake Michigan.
SAL. Dianah . . .

(*She starts to exit.* SAL *follows her like a puppy. Suddenly* YOVAN *rushes out onto the street running directly toward her. He's carrying in his hand an old-fashioned looking bomb, a round black thing with a long fuse. The fuse is burning. He is heading toward* CHRIS'S *apartment window with it. But . . . when he sees* DIANAH, *he stops in his tracks. She sees him. She stops in hers. It's love at first sight. Only* SAL *seems worried but who hears* SAL.)

SAL. Dianah, the man's got a bomb.

(*Nobody hears him.*)

YOVAN. Allo there, stranger lady.
DIANAH. Hello . . . there.

(*If* YOVAN *prides himself on being tough, he also
    prides himself on being suave. The man of many
    moves. The fuse is burning, but he only has eyes for*
    DIANAH. SAL *only has eyes for the fuse.*)

YOVAN. Stranger lady, you are beautiful. No, not just
beautiful, you are cute.
DIANAH. It takes a very secure man these days to
acknowledge beauty in a woman. Most men feel
threatened by us.
YOVAN. Most men are chupped liver. Such is not the
case in my case.

(*In a very sensual gesture, he bites the fuse off just
    before it is to explode the bomb.*)

DIANAH. Were you going to . . . (*She gestures to the
bomb*)
YOVAN. Yes, I was going to blow up a person's apart-
ment. Maybe blow up person inside.
DIANAH. You're an anarchist?
YOVAN. I am Man. Man is everything.
DIANAH. And woman?
YOVAN. Woman is everything plus something else to
boot. This . . . this is a dangerous neighborhood. I do
not want to scare the pants off you . . . but you should
not be out alone.
SAL. She's not alone. She's with me.

(*Nobody, needless to say, hears him.*)

DIANAH. (*Very triste*) Sometimes, it's best to be alone.

SAL. You're not alone.

DIANAH. We come into this world alone and we go out alone.

SAL. I have nothing more to say on the subject.

YOVAN. Are you, eh, visiting for somebody or are you, eh, shooting the brizz as they say?

DIANAH. I am mourning. A person I loved died. He died in front of my eyes, so to speak.

YOVAN. It is tough to be lonely. But when the going gets to be tough cookies, my cookies do not crumble, if you know what I mean.

DIANAH. It is clear that you have hot blood in your veins. A woman can tell such things. I, on the other hand, am frigid, so to speak.

YOVAN. Alaska is frigid too. But I tell you this, underknitt your frozen tundra there is oil vating to flow.

SAL. I don't believe this.

DIANAH. Excuse me for asking, but you're not a native of these parts. Your accent . . .

YOVAN. Is true. I am in Chicago only ten years. Originally I am from Cleveland.

DIANAH. I seem to detect a scent of mimeo ink on you.

YOVAN. Your nose is a credit to your brain. I print menus on mimeo machine and I also print Serbian newspaper in my basement. I call it Serbian Sun. I write powerful stuff. I write: America, wake up. People need you. My friends. They give up. They go back to the old country. So I write: Fooey on you, you chupped liver patriots. Fooey on your kids. Fooey on your family. Stuff like that I write. Leaflets too.

DIANAH. I used to write leaflets. Oh, those were the days, my friend, we thought they'd never end . . .

YOVAN. Yes, we'd sing and dance forever and a day
. . .

DIANAH. We'd lead the life we choose. We'd fight
and never lose . . . (*She starts crying*)

YOVAN. Oh, veep no more my lady. Veep no more today. It is not time to give up. America needs us. We
must link up hands and arms and feet and hearts and do
big stuff.

DIANAH. Hope stirs in my bosom again.

YOVAN. Something stirs in me, too. My name is
Yovan.

DIANAH. My name is Dianah.

SAL. My name is Sal.

YOVAN. My place is not far away.

SAL. That line about the frozen tundra was mine
. . . Dianah . . .

(*All go Off.* CHRIS *enters his apartment, holding the car
top. He doesn't know what to do with it. He is
tired. He looks around and throws car top in the
corner of the room right on top of the pile of rags
that is* ROGER. *A groan is heard.* CHRIS *is startled.
He listens. He hears nothing. He closes the door.
Another groan is heard. The car top moves.* CHRIS
*turns around. He either thinks he is hearing things
or there's a prowler in the house.*)

CHRIS. Who's there? Who are you?

(*From underneath the car top the head of the old man
emerges.* ROGER *is a little groggy from sleep and a
little groggy from the hit in the head with a car
top.*)

ROGER. Chris, Chris. It's me. Take me back, Chris.

CHRIS. Hey, who the hell are you?

(*There is dead silence. Then* ROGER *softly, very softly and through sobs, begins singing:* "*All we are saying is . . .*")

Give me a break.

ROGER. It's me, Chris.

CHRIS. Me who?

ROGER. It's me. Roger. You remember Roger O'Dwyer. Your old comrade from the Sixties.

CHRIS. I remember Roger. You're not Roger. I know Roger and I don't know you. I don't know how you know me but I do know I don't know you. Who are you?

(ROGER, *although hurt by not being remembered, understands. He in effect now has to audition for* CHRIS *to show him he is who he says he is.*)

ROGER. Hey, hey, L.B.J. (*Pause*)
Ho, Ho, Ho-Chi-Minh! (*Pause*)
Hi, Hi, Chou-En-lai!

CHRIS. ROGER!

ROGER. Chris!

(CHRIS *offers to shake hands, but* ROGER *wants to do "the old hand shake."* CHRIS *has forgotten how to do it but they muddle through somehow ending up in an embrace.* ROGER *doesn't want to let go of the embrace.* CHRIS *has to peel him off. Although* CHRIS *is feeling slightly more in control his feet are hardly on the ground.*)

CHRIS. Roger. It's you, I know . . . but . . . I mean, the last time I saw you . . . you were . . . well . . . frankly, you were my age.

ROGER. I'm still your age, Chris.

CHRIS. Hell, Rog, let's call a spade a spade. You look like an old man, man.

ROGER. Oh, right! I keep forgetting! Underneath all this stuff I look fine. (*He takes wig off. Reveals old* ROG) Not that I have a right to look fine. But I do.

CHRIS. So, why the disguise, Rog? You hiding from somebody?

ROGER. From "them."

CHRIS. "Them," eh?

ROGER. Yeah, "them."

CHRIS. Do I know any of "them"?

ROGER. You know all of "them." Goddamn women and their goddamn orgasms. So you were down screaming at the cops, eh? Like in the old days, right Chris?

CHRIS. It was a little different this time.

ROGER. Sure it was. You were by yourself. Alone! But proud! You are alone no more, you majestic son of a bitch, you. I've come to join you. You didn't think I'd remember, did you?

(CHRIS *obviously feels that* ROGER *has lost his mind.*)

CHRIS. Remember what Rog?

ROGER. Don't tease me, Chris. I'm not that bad. The Big Meeting, Chris. The LAST BIG MEETING before The Big Split.

CHRIS. And . . . eh . . . what happened at the Last Big Meeting?

ROGER. You remember. Everybody was there. Jerry Rubin, Abbie Hoffman, Tom Hayden, Rennie Davis, Mark Rudd, J.B. Kellogg, you, me, and "them."

"They" were there too. Remember? The Days of Rage were over. Nobody had any rage left. Nobody had any grass even. The movement was over, we all felt. I was like the last supper. And then Abbie had an idea? The last brilliant idea he was to have. Dear Abbie. Remember? He said that we should split up but plan to return. Return to Chicago at the dawn of the new decade, and, if nothing else, as a gesture of our continuing protest, we would march once again and puke on the foul system. Days of Vomit, Abbie called them. Oh Chris! Everybody forgot! Nobody came except for you! When I saw your picture in the papers puking alone, I wanted to kill myself! You! Alone! You did it alone but you did it!

CHRIS. Oh, Rog, Rog, you can't be serious, man.

ROGER. You're all that's left. You're the only one. YOU ARE THE MOVEMENT NOW. (*He falls on his knees*) Take me back! Forgive me, Chris, for I have sinned, but take me back! PLEASE!

CHRIS. Rog. Rog. Hey . . . I can't take you back . . . You don't understand.

ROGER. NO, YOU DON'T UNDERSTAND! I was going to kill myself. I bought the pills. I wrote my suicide notes. I was going to die and then I saw you puking in the papers, and you gave me hope. If you don't take me back, I'll kill myself.

CHRIS. Rog, I can't.

(ROGER *opens the bottle of pills. Empties it in his mouth.* CHRIS *tries to stop him.* ROGER *throws him back.* CHRIS *is frantic.*)

ROGER! OH MY GOD! I AM THE MOVEMENT! I TAKE YOU BACK!

(ROGER *rushes toward him spitting out the pills into* CHRIS'S *face. Embraces him.*)

ROGER. You saved my life! (*Breaks away from the embrace*) Why? Why did you save my life? I don't deserve it. You should spit on me! Go ahead, spit on me!

CHRIS. I can't spit, Rog. I am very, very tired. I'll spit on you later, I promise.

ROGER. You'll spit on me when I tell you what I've done.

CHRIS. Don't tell me, Rog.

ROGER. I have to. You have to know the scum that you're taking back.

CHRIS. Give me a break, Rog. Don't tell me.

ROGER. I've done it all, baby. From A to Z, but we'll start in the middle with M for marriage. Married. Me! Yes. Last year, I married this girl named Nadja. I bought a car! Me! A car! A Buick, Chris! Spit on me. Spit at will, Chris. And in my rec room, YES, I HAD A REC ROOM. And in my rec room, I had a letter framed that was printed in the T.V. GUIDE. Concerned viewer writes. I complained because they cancelled my favorite T.V. show. (*Real anguish, real self-loathing and self-lacerating*) I HAD A FAVORITE T.V. SHOW! Hit me! Hurt me! And then my wife left me. The whole middle class shebang, Chris. Do you know why she left me? Because of orgasms. Yes. She wasn't getting enough orgasms. And that's when it hit me! That's when it dawned on me. It's the women that killed the movement! They did it. We never should have told them about orgasms. They didn't know. Why did we tell them. Now they all want them. And not just on May Day, Chris. Every month they want one or two. Yes. Orgasms! And they got us convinced that we should be giving them orgasms! And while we were wondering how to give it to them so they like it they took over the movement. They formed their own movement! Remember J.B. Kellogg? He got a sex change I hear just so he could join the radical wing of NOW. Radical wing. Chris! Are you listening? The women! They've got internal struggles for power. They've got splinter groups. They've got radical wings. They've got all the good shit we used to have! And what are we doing? What are the guys doing? We're wondering why we can't give them orgasms. It's a conspiracy, Chris. They suppress their orgasms on purpose just to confuse us. They've got us shaving twice a day and they're not shaving at all. They've raised our consciousness and lowered our cocks and they want to know why we can't give them an orgasm. They've got us by the balls and they're saying "nuts" to us. Orgasms! Orgasms! IF I HAD AN ORGASM I'D GIVE IT TO THEM JUST SO THEY'D LEAVE ME ALONE!

(*He is spent. He falls down on the floor from sheer exhaustion.* CHRIS *seems catatonic.* ROGER *speaks again. Slowly now. The hysteria has passed.*)

That's why I put on this wig and stuff. I feel safe. Women don't bother me. They don't expect anything from an old man. I'm a sexual incognito.

(*Becomes old man. He looks at* CHRIS. *At his apartment. At what is left of* CHRIS' *car. He is full of admiration.*)

But enough about me. You! You're the one! You've remained pure! Look at you. Still the shabby wrinkled clothes. You're probably broke. No job. No wife. Nothing! What's your secret, Chris?!

(CHRIS *is weary of all this.*)

CHRIS. Either you have it or you don't.

(ROGER *alludes to the car top.*)

ROGER. That's classic! Walking around the city with that! Mocking our car crazy society. You magnificent son of a bitch. How, Chris, how?
CHRIS. I have to lie down now, Rog.
ROGER. You go right ahead, man.

(CHRIS *flops down on sofa.* ROGER *gives him the power sign.*)

Dream on, man!

(NADJA *appears on the street and heads toward* CHRIS' *apartment.* ROGER *goes to the window. Looks out. Alarm clock goes off!* CHRIS *sits up a little and looks at* ROGER *looking out of the window.*)

CHRIS. Rog. I haven't got the strength to explain but you should move away from the window.
ROGER. Why's that, buddy?

(NADJA *knocks on the door and just as she does a huge rolled up newspaper flies through the window and hits* ROGER *smack in the face. He staggers, falls down, and hits his head. Goes out like a light.* CHRIS *gets up slowly to get the door.* NADJA *knocks. Silence.* NADJA *knocks again.*)

CHRIS. I'm coming.

(*He opens the door.* NADJA *is there in a bright halter,
    shorts and chain belt. She looks at* CHRIS. CHRIS
    looks at her. CHRIS *is so exhausted he looks and
    acts like an old man.*)

NADJA. So, you're old man Chris. You don't look so
bad for an old man, pops.
CHRIS. Thank you. It's how you feel that counts.
And I feel very old.
NADJA. Don't worry. I'll fix that in no time at all.

(*She starts undressing.* CHRIS *watches her for a while.*)

CHRIS. Who are you?
NADJA. (*She goes into her act*) That's up to you, ac-
tually. I could be a visiting nurse, no? What about one
of those meals on wheels women, huh? I know. A
granddaughter? Incest is making a comeback, gramps?
But where will I sleep, Grampa. There's only one bed.
(*She looks at him*) You're supposed to chortle now and
say: Why don't we sleep together.
CHRIS. Look, kid, I'm too old for this game.
NADJA. No you're not. You, hell, you couldn't be a
day over fifty.
CHRIS. I'm thirty-seven, dammit.
NADJA. Sorry, Arnold told me you were touchy
about your age.
CHRIS. Who's Arnold?
NADJA. Arnold the pimp.
CHRIS. Oh, the pimp! Oh, I get it. You're one of Ar-
nold's girls.
NADJA. No, Arnold's one of my pimps.
CHRIS. Who cares.
NADJA. I care.
CHRIS. The point is you're a prostitute.

NADJA. No, I'm not. I'm a slut. Prostitutes do it just for the money. I do it as a political statement as well.

CHRIS. Oh, please. No statements. Look, kid, I'm broke. I got no money.

NADJA. That's all right. You're paid up for the year.

CHRIS. I never paid for it.

NADJA. So it was a gift subscription.

CHRIS. Look, the old man who lived here died.

(NADJA *sees* ROGER *and screams.*)

NADJA. Is that him?

CHRIS. No, he's not an old man.

(NADJA *looks at him again. Then at* CHRIS.)

NADJA. But he's dead.

CHRIS. No, he's not dead.

NADJA. What's the matter with him.

(CHRIS *has no energy to explain.*)

CHRIS. Would you believe me if I told you the evening news hit him real hard?

NADJA. Is he the old man I was supposed to do it with?

CHRIS. Yeah, sure.

NADJA. We almost had something going at his expense, eh? Too bad. (*She starts putting on her clothes*)

CHRIS. How old are you?

NADJA. Nineteen.

CHRIS. When I was nineteen . . .

NADJA. I know! I know! You were probably trying to save the world and all.

CHRIS. Well, as a matter of fact . . .

NADJA. Yeah, yeah, I've heard it all before. My husband was a world saver. Where did it get him?

CHRIS. You're married?

NADJA. Divorced.

CHRIS. Where's your husband?

NADJA. I don't know. Lying around somewhere. You married?

CHRIS. I'm getting divorced.

NADJA. It's all crap, isn't it?

CHRIS. Well, it's what it is.

NADJA. Crap. That's what it is.

CHRIS. It's what we make it, right?

NADJA. Right, and we make it crap.

CHRIS. Stop saying "crap."

NADJA. Don't tell me what to do. Nobody tells me what to do.

CHRIS. Nobody's telling you what to do.

(*Silence.*)

NADJA. It's crap. That's what life is. A big crap trap.

CHRIS. All right. All right. I get the message. So it's bad.

NADJA. It's not bad. It's nothing. Zero. Pointless. Empty.

CHRIS. You sound like Goldie Hawn in a Bergman movie. You're too damned young to be so cynical.

NADJA. Oh, yeah.

CHRIS. Yeah. Things change.

NADJA. For the worse.

CHRIS. Not necessarily. It's just . . . well . . . it's the times we're in, that's all. Everybody's just thinking about themselves. Me. Me. Me.

NADJA. And what're you thinking about?

(CHRIS *is angry at having no comeback.*)

CHRIS. That's not the point.

NADJA. What is the point?

CHRIS. The point is . . . I'm in my thirties. But you, hell. Nineteen. When I was nineteen . . .

NADJA. Oh yeah, and where did it get you?

CHRIS. Get me? I'll tell you where it got me. Right here. (*Pounds his chest*) At least I tried. At least I felt something once.

NADJA. I feel for you.

CHRIS. No, I feel for you kid!

NADJA. I don't want you to feel for me.

CHRIS. That's just too bad, isn't it. Because I feel for you.

NADJA. Feel for yourself, sucker.

CHRIS. I've felt for myself already today. Now I'm going to feel for you. Boy, do I feel for you.

(*She swings her purse at him. He ducks. She is ready to cry.*)

NADJA. You no good hypocrite. Just because you've done your bit in the past doesn't mean you can feel superior to me. You no good bastard. You're just as bad as my husband, Roger. He wanted me to be his little woman. My father, Yovan, wanted me to be his little girl. A whore, that's all you men want. Well, I will not be a whore. I'm a slut.

(*She's bawling. She starts to leave.* CHRIS *tries to stop her. She exits, slams door. Window shuts.* CHRIS *opens door, goes out into hallway.*)

CHRIS. Wait! What's your name?

(ROGER *wakes suddenly.*)

ROGER. Nadja! Revenge! I smell Revenge!

(NADJA *is gone.* CHRIS *goes back into his apartment.*)

ROGER. Oh, Chris. I had a terrible nightmare. Thank God I'm here. Where is my box? I need my box!
CHRIS. I don't know, Rog. What box?
ROGER. My box, I need my box. I need my song. Oh Chris!

(*He leaps for his bag. Pulls out his box. He turns on cassette. "THOSE WERE THE DAYS." Clutches it to his heart like a Bible. Hugs* CHRIS. *This time* CHRIS *hugs him back.*)

CHRIS. There, there Rog. It's all right.

(MRS. BRUCHINSKI *enters.*)

MRS. BRUCHINSKI. I got the blues in the night.
ROGER. Oh Chris, remember the old days.
MRS. BRUCHINSKI. I remember. I was young in the old days.
ROGER. And I was a rebel with a cause. I was going to change the world.
MRS. BRUCHINSKI. Instead the world changed us. Oh, so sad.
ROGER. Oh, yes. So sad.

(ROGER *and* MRS. BRUCHINSKI *cry.*)

CHRIS. Oh, my God. C'mon. Don't cry. It's over. When it's over, it's over . . . and it's over.
ROGER. I had a life . . . and it's gone.
MRS. BRUCHINSKI. I had a baby boy . . . and he's gone.

CHRIS. We should all go . . . it's late.

MRS. BRUCHINSKI. Wonderful dreams I remember . . . People in the streets . . . songs in the air.

ROGER. And in the darkest night the burning issues of the day lit up the way for us and we could see the New Dawn. Oh, Chris. Oh, world. Oh, life.

(ROGER *and* MRS. BRUCHINSKI *weep on* CHRIS *shoulder.*)

CHRIS. Oh, Rog.

MRS. BRUCHINSKI. Oh, my gosh.

(*The three of them embrace each other. We hear a heart-rending renidition of "THOSE WERE THE DAYS." CHRIS breaks away, picks up typewriter and paper, goes out on "stoop" and sits. Lights fade slowly.*)

END OF ACT I

ACT II

(*Out in the street we hear a loud siren going by and as it starts to fade* SAL *runs out onto the street. He howls like a young King Lear who's had a vision of his older years and stops.* SAL *is wearing only a flasher's raincoat. He jumps around like a desperate man "flashing" the city. His efforts, energetic and manic to begin with, depress him. He stops.*)

SAL. Just as I thought. Nobody looks. I've bared my soul, and now I've bared my body. The results are in. I don't exist. (*He cries in agony*) SOMEBODY HELP ME! I'M A MAN IN THE STREET! SOMEBODY INTERVIEW ME! I'M A REAL NICE GUY! YOU DON'T HAVE TO LOVE ME! YOU DON'T EVEN HAVE TO LIKE ME! I'LL TAKE HATE! Today is the worst day of the rest of my life. (*He runs Off*)

(*Lights come up in the apartment. It's a crack before the crack of dawn.* CHRIS *is typing his apology.* ROGER *is asleep on the floor nearby.* CHRIS *reads what He has written.*)

CHRIS. Looking back on that time I now feel . . . (*He looks out thinking. He types over what he has written. Writes again*) That whole period of my life seems like a long nightmare from which I have irrevocably awakened. (*He continues typing*)
ROGER. (*Singing*) "All we are saying . . ."
CHRIS. Shut up, Rog.

46

ROGER. "Is give peace a chance . . ."
CHRIS. Give me a break, Rog. Shut up. (CHRIS *types.*
A short silence)
ROGER. "All we are saying . . ."
CHRIS. You've said it already, dammit.
ROGER. "Is give peace a chance . . ."

(CHRIS *types "give peace a chance." Realizing his error*
     he types over it.)

CHRIS. Shut up. The war is over! It's all over. Even
Pete Seeger's winding down.

                    (ROGER *snores.*)

I'm apologizing for what we did, Rog, so I can keep my
job. That's what I'm doing. (*He types. Short silence*)
ROGER. "All we are saying . . ."

(CHRIS *can't take it. Jumps up and kicks the rubble on*
     the floor that is ROGER.

CHRIS. Shut up! Shut up!

(ROGER *shuts up. Starts snoring.* CHRIS *goes back to*
     the typewriter.)

ROGER. "We shall overcome . . ."

(CHRIS *drops his head on the typewriter. From across*
     the hall he hears MRS. BRUCHINSKI.)

MRS. BRUCHINSKI. (*Offstage*) "We shall overcome
. . ."

(*She opens the door singing and steps into* CHRIS'
apartment singing. ROGER *is asleep singing. She is
at the door. A short duet.*)

ROGER & MRS. BRUCHINSKI. "We shall overcome
. . . some . . . day . . ."

(CHRIS *looks at both of them.*)

CHRIS. I live here. This is my place. It's the 80's not
the 60's. I insist on that.

(*They stop singing.* ROGER *snores.*)

MRS. BRUCHINSKI. I couldn't sleep. I get blues in the
night again. And then I hear song and I come . . . It is
song of my heart, Kris. We sing it again.
CHRIS. I don't want to sing anymore . . . I've sung
them all, Mrs. Bruchinski . . . peace songs . . . protest
songs . . . pollution songs . . . I've sung, I've hummed.
I've carried the ball, the poster and the tune . . .
MRS. BRUCHINSKI. (*Jumps in*) Yes, me too. And it
was wonderful. One more time again we sing . . . we
climb the mountain, Chris.
CHRIS. There are no mountains in Chicago, Mrs.
Bruchinski.
MRS. BRUCHINSKI. Hope is mountain, Chris. Even in
Chicago there is hope. We climb the mountain and we
sing and together we overcome misery and despair. We
overcome trouble and bad life and we overcome disco
music too.
CHRIS. That's a helluva lot to overcome.
MRS. BRUCHINSKI. That's right. We better start right
away before there's helluva lot more. I stay here and not
budge till I hear you sing.

CHRIS. All right. All right.

(CHRIS *escorts* MRS. BRUCHINSKI *back to her apartment singing "WE SHALL OVERCOME."* ROGER, *in his sleep, joins in.* BETTY *enters on the street and hears them.*)

BETTY. I never thought I'd hear it again!

(MRS. BRUCHINSKI *walks into her apartment.* CHRIS *closes the door and reenters his apartment, leaning on door frame, singing.*)

CHRIS. "We shall overcome . . . some da-a-a-ay . . ."

(BETTY *joins him in singing out in the street, wiping a tear that's making her mascara run.* ROGER *sings in his sleep. It's a trio. The song is even getting to* CHRIS, *but when he finishes, in the total silence that follows, he quickly pulls himself out of it and rushes back to his typewriter.*)

MRS. BRUCHINSKI. (*Offstage*) THANK YOU, KRIS!
CHRIS. (*Softly*) You're welcome.
MRS. BRUCHINSKI. (*Offstage*) I SAID "THANK YOU, KRIS!"
CHRIS. I SAID "YOU'RE WELCOME!"
MRS. BRUCHINSKI. (*Offstage*) DON'T MENTION IT!

(*He tries to go back to the typewriter.* BETTY *stands where she has stood still lost in the emotion of the song. She cries out as if calling the ghosts from the past.*)

BETTY. Stokely! Eldridge!

(ROGER *sits up suddenly. He could be awake or asleep.*)

ROGER. Rennie Davis! Tom Hayden! Billy Kunstler!

(CHRIS, *without so much as a thought, slugs him.*
BETTY *strolls Off, full of nostalgia.* ROGER'S
nightmare continues.)

Orgasms! Orgasms! They're everywhere. The women!
We thought we had free love in the 60's. It wasn't free.
They're sending us the bill in the 80's and we gotta pay!
CHRIS. ROGER. ROGER. Wake up! You're having a
nightmare. You're giving me a nightmare!
ROGER. MT. ST. HELENS IS ONE OF THEM! IT'S
A WOMAN VOLCANO! The women! The mountains
named after guys are doing nothing. Mt. McKinley. Mt.
Washington. Pikes Peak. Nothing. They're all dormant
and doing zilch, but HELENS . . . is thundering away.
The goddamn mountain is having an orgasm! It's a
cosmic orgasm, and now they'll expect me to top that if
I want to be a man. I can't top that. I can't top that!

(ROGER *falls, exhausted.* NADJA *appears on the street
and heads straight for* CHRIS' *building. She knocks
on the door.*)

CHRIS. Go back to sleep, Mrs. Bruchinski. I sang to
you once already. What do you want from me?

(NADJA *knocks.*)

All right. All right.

(*Goes toward the door singing rapidly and angrily: "WE SHALL OVERCOME." Opens the door. Stops singing when he sees* NADJA *who is now wearing a skirt.*)

NADJA. Boy, you never give up do you. Once a radical always a radical.

(CHRIS *is a little confused. Goes with it.*)

CHRIS. Yeah, it's in my blood so to speak. Come on in.

NADJA. I couldn't sleep. I've been thinking about what you said. About life.

CHRIS. Yeah, I've been thinking about life too. It's all crap.

NADJA. Don't make fun of me.

CHRIS. I'm not. You were right. It's all crap.

NADJA. Lay off, will you! It's easy for you. You have hopes and dreams and all that stuff and I . . . I don't want to make any excuses for myself but I was just a kid when all that stuff was going on. I didn't know I was missing out on something. So I want the truth. I know it's crap now but was it ever better?

CHRIS. You really want the truth?

NADJA. Hey, what do you think I want: A pair of blue eyes and a smile. I'm a slut. I eat truth for breakfast. I can take it.

CHRIS. It was the worst of times and it was the best of times. (*He pauses*) That was a joke.

NADJA. I didn't come here for laughs. If you're not going to take me seriously.

(*She starts to leave. He stops her.*)

CHRIS. I'll tell you how it was. You knew who the good guys were and you knew who the bad guys were and you knew which one you wanted to be. It was black and white. Now it's grey. People had jobs, they had homes and mortgages and bills to pay, but there was something bigger to worry about and think about that made those small everyday worries bearable. People were not afraid or ashamed to take sides. And both sides went to great extremes to prove a simple point that they loved their country. We were all impatient because we had a feeling, a stupid feeling, that if we could just think of something truly splendid . . . we could make it come true that instant. And I remember going up on a platform . . . I too had a vision . . . a sea of people stood before me . . . My mind went completely blank. I didn't know what to say. So I called out to them . . . almost calling for help . . . CITIZENS OF THE UNITED STATES OF AMERICA . . . And the crowd roared back. I can't remember what I said to them but I do remember that I was there. I spoke my piece. I shared my vision. And I was young.

(NADJA *is in tears. Loud crying.*)

NADJA. I was only seven years old, then.
CHRIS. Well, we're both grown up now.
NADJA. Thank God it wasn't all just crap from start to finish. (*She's really crying*) All right. You've convinced me. That's it. Boy, oh boy, that is it. I don't know what you have in mind but if you want to make things better, I'm with you. Sign me up.
CHRIS. Oh God, now I've done it. (*He sits.*)
NADJA. The only other person who talks like you is my father, Yovan. And I ran away from him. He stays up late at night and types too. Same kind of stuff

probably as yours. Full of hope and dreams and stuff
like that. Can I read what you've written?

(*She heads for the typewriter.* CHRIS *jumps up to inter-
cede.*)

CHRIS. No, not that. It's . . . uh . . . uh . . . not finished. (*He hides the typing.*) I'll give you some . . . uh . . .
some of my old stuff.

(*He runs around looking for it.* NADJA *looks at* ROGER.
ROGER *snores.*)

Oh! It's so nice to see somebody who still lives with his
father.

(CHRIS *finds an old speech of his. Brings it to her. He
feels guilty and trapped. Gives her his old speech.*)

CHRIS. Here, read.

(NADJA *settles down with the speech.* CHRIS *sits at the
typewriter and looks at her. Just as she begins to
read* ROGER *lets out a snatch of song in his sleep
. . .*)

ROGER. "All we are saying . . ."
NADJA. Like father like son.

(CHRIS *looks at her across his typewriter. He is falling
in love. She looks up and sees him looking at her.
She then looks down at the pages again.* CHRIS *continues staring. Out in the street we hear a howl of
loneliness and then see* SAL *enter. He is what he is
only more so by now.* SAL *is "flashing" the en-
virons, crying, singing.*)

SAL. Sal, Sal, huckleberry Sal
Never knew a sweeter guy
Don't think I ever shall . . .

(*He can't sing anymore. But he can flash.* BETTY *the cop appears. Sees him.*)

BETTY. Hey, you! What the hell you think you're doing!
SAL. I am exposing what's left of myself.
BETTY. And I'm proposing you stop exposing or I'm going to start imposing.
SAL. If you were really there you wouldn't be talking to me.
BETTY. I am talking to you, buddy.

(SAL *gets stabbed in the heart by this word.*)

SAL. Buddy! I've always wanted to be somebody's buddy.

(BETTY *is softening a little.*)

BETTY. You're in a bad way, pal.

(SAL *gets stabbed in the heart again.*)

SAL. Don't call me pal, if you don't mean it. Don't tease me, please.
BETTY. Man, I thought I was lonely and insecure.
SAL. Loneliness and insecurity were my happy period.

(SAL *cries.* BETTY *goes up to him and starts buttoning his overcoat.*)

BETTY. Has anybody ever told you that you're kind of cute when you cry?

SAL. No never. (SAL *cries*)

BETTY. You are. You really are.

(SAL *cries*.)

Oh, come on. It's not your fault that you're suffering.

SAL. It's not. Whose fault is it?

BETTY. It's our fault.

SAL. Thank God.

BETTY. Everybody has let you down. I look at you and I see where we have failed. You are a living example that the human potential movement didn't work. That the alternate life style movement didn't work. That the cults and the crazes and conscience expanding drugs didn't work. Nothing has worked for you.

SAL. No, not a thing.

BETTY. You know what you are?

SAL. No, tell me!

BETTY. You're the Little Guy. The Republicans, the Democrats, the Socialists . . . they all talk about reaching the little guy and you're him. You're the Little Guy himself. And nobody has reached you.

SAL. Nobody even calls.

BETTY. And yet your lonely suffering is not for naught.

SAL. What's it for?

BETTY. You are a measure of how far we still have to go. You, Little Guy, are the one whose heart and soul we have to reach if we are to realize the dream of humanity. It's up to me . . . up to us . . . The women's movement is your last chance . . . our last chance . . . to reach the little guy of history. Reach the little guy. Reach the little guy. I am reaching out to you. Here is my hand, Little Guy. It's a woman's hand . . . It's black and it's beautiful and it needs you. Take it!

SAL. I'll take it.

BETTY. (*Chants*) Reach the Little Guy. Reach the Little Guy.

(*He crawls to* BETTY.)

SAL. Oh, I'm weak with hope.

(BETTY *picks him up in her arms.*)

Oh, my God. I'm being picked up. I've never been picked up before.

BETTY. My place is not far away.

SAL. Wait. I have to tell you something. I think I'm Jewish.

BETTY. All I now is that you're a cute and lonely, little guy.

SAL. Wait. I have to tell you something else. I'm a . . . virgin.

BETTY. I just became a virgin myself.

(*They look at each other. She starts carrying him Offstage.* YOVAN *runs onto the street. Stops in his tracks when he sees them.*)

YOVAN. Stop! My hat off to you police woman person. It brings tears to my eyeballs to see Black and White get along so nifty. You are a credit to your racial quota.

(SAL *mouths "thank you."* BETTY *carries* SAL *Off.* YOVAN *looks after them.*)

Only in America!

(NADJA, *having finished reading* CHRIS' *speech, clutches it to her bosom and lets out a cry of joy.*)

NADJA. It's so beautiful!

(YOVAN *goes to the payphone. Looks for a number. He is carrying an attache case with him, and God only knows what's inside.* CHRIS *embraces* NADJA.)

CHRIS. It's an old speech . . . I mean . . . it's kind of dated, don't you think.

NADJA. No, it'll never be dated. You're really something.

CHRIS. Yeah, the question is what?

(YOVAN *dials.* CHRIS' *telephone rings.* CHRIS *picks it up.*)

Hello.

YOVAN. Allo, buster boy.

CHRIS. Oh, no. It's not you again, is it?

YOVAN. Yes, it is me, Redical of the Sixties. I give you new offer. Since you do not come to the New World, I bring New World to you. I have in my possession two stuffed cabbages a la Serb and one Polaroid Pronto. You can go yummy, yummy in the privacy of your rotten apartment. I shoot you with Polaroid Pronto.

CHRIS. No, you won't.

YOVAN. Then I shoot you with gun. You are not going to make uncle of monkey out of me. Good-bye. Next time you see me you will be dead. (YOVAN *hangs up*)

NADJA. Who was that?

CHRIS. Nobody you'd know.

NADJA. I have to go. I want to find my father and tell him about you.

CHRIS. He doesn't know you're a . . .

NADJA. A slut. No, he'd kill me if he knew. He'd kill you, too.

CHRIS. I already have a guy that wants to kill me.

(YOVAN *is pacing down in the street. He is working himself up.* NADJA *hugs* CHRIS. NADJA *kisses* CHRIS.)

NADJA. Thank you. I'll be back.

(YOVAN *is coming up the stairs.*)

I'll make it up to my father. I've hurt him without even knowing it.

(*She bursts out of the door in a fit of eagerness to start a new life just as* YOVAN *reaches the landing. The door opens and slams him right in the face. He staggers back against the wall as* NADJA *runs down the stairs and falls out cold on the floor.* CHRIS *goes and shuts the door without seeing him.* CHRIS *is feeling dreadful. An imposter. He has conned the girl into thinking he is somebody he's not. He's trapped in that role and he doesn't like it. In the end it's all* ROGER'S *fault. It it hadn't been for him . . .* ROGER *stirs in his sleep.*)

ROGER. "What do we want?"

CHRIS. I want you out of here!

ROGER. "When do we want it?"

CHRIS. Now! It's all your fault. Why the hell did you have to show up when you did? Why?

ROGER. "All we are saying . . ."

(CHRIS *screams out in frustration. Can't take it. It's almost the last straw. He starts throwing stuff on top of* ROGER. *Anything he can find. A pillow. Throws the rug on top of him. Puts the remainder of the car on top of him just so he won't hear that song anymore. He is out of breath and shaking with anger by the time he is finished but at least it's silent. He listens. No, he can't hear* ROGER. *He heads for the typewriter. The rubble that is* ROGER *stirs.*)

ROGER. (*Singing*) "Chicago, Chicago."

(CHRIS *goes crazy. He jumps on top of the rubble ready to choke him.*)

CHRIS. SHUT UP! SHUT UP! SHUT UP!

(ROGER *wakes up.*)

ROGER. (*Sees the rubble on top of himself.*) Thanks for tucking me in, Chris. How's the proclamation coming along?

CHRIS. What proclamation!

ROGER. When I went to sleep you were typing the Proclamation of the Second Movement.

CHRIS. ROG! There is no proclamation. There is no second movement. Listen to me, man, and listen well. I've gathered all your sleeping pills and stuff so don't try to pull any of that suicide crap on me. This has gone far enough.

ROGER. I KNEW IT! I KNEW IT WAS TOO GOOD TO BE TRUE! YOU'RE KICKING ME OUT! OUT OF THE MOVEMENT!

(*There is a movement on the landing.* YOVAN *is reviving a little.*)

I'LL KILL MYSELF! (He *scrounges around and pulls out something*)
    CHRIS. What's that?
    ROGER. Rat poison!

(CHRIS *throws himself on top of* ROGER *trying to get it away.* YOVAN *manages to get on his feet outside. He staggers a little forward. Just as he does* MRS. BRUCHINSKI *opens the door and catches him flat on the face.* YOVAN *goes down again. She goes right past him without seeing him and opens* CHRIS' *door. She stands there and sees* CHRIS *lying on top of* ROGER, *struggling with him.*)

ROGER. I love you, Chris.
CHRIS. I know. I know.
ROGER. But you don't love me.
CHRIS. I do too. I love you.

(ROGER *embraces* CHRIS. CHRIS *can't but embrace him back.* YOVAN *is rising slowly.* MRS. BRUCHINSKI *just shakes her head at the sight of the two men hugging and starts to leave. Flings the door open. Catches* YOVAN *on the face and plasters him against the wall again. She stands on the landing shaking her head. Looks at* CHRIS' *door. She sighs and goes into her place again.* YOVAN *is back on the floor again.* CHRIS *is tucking* ROGER *in again.*)

Rog, I've got something to tell you. For the sake of the Second Movement, I think we should split up.

ROGER. Split up?

CHRIS. Yes, you should go to Los Angeles and start things out there, while I carry on here in Chicago.

ROGER. And leave you, Chris!

CHRIS. Yes, leave me, Rog. Leave me. Please.

ROGER. I'm scared of L.A., Chris. Look what it did to Tom Hayden.

CHRIS. All the more reason for you to go. They need somebody like you out there.

ROGER. Oh, Chris. I don't even know what the burning issue of the day is anymore.

CHRIS. Sure you do, Rog.

ROGER. I sure don't, Chris. I was hoping you knew. What's the word, Chris? What's the burning issue of the day?

CHRIS. What it's always been, Rog. When the world we envision is better than the one we live in, then we must follow our vision.

ROGER. Because that's the kind of guys we are. Right, Chris?

CHRIS. Right, Rog.

ROGER. All right, I'll go. I'm scared of L.A., but I'll go. Oh, Chris. Wasn't it wonderful when we were young and loved what we did. Wasn't it?

CHRIS. Yes, it was. And now we're older . . .

ROGER. And now we hate ourselves. Why?

CHRIS. Because we quit.

ROGER. I quit. Not you. You didn't quit. That's why I love you . . . you . . . Remember in Spartacus . . . when Tony Curtis was dying and he hugged Kirk Douglas. I'm the Tony Curtis here and you're Kirk. I love you Spartacus. Good-bye. (ROGER *goes to bedroom to pack up and go*)

(CHRIS *goes to the typewriter.* YOVAN, *his bearings lost, staggers up to his feet and goes right for the door. It's* MRS. BRUCHINSKI *door.*)

YOVAN. I fix your goose for good now!

(*He charges into her apartment. A scream is heard. Then a loud resounding bang. Then a groan!* CHRIS *continues typing.* MRS. BRUCHINSKI'S *door flings open and* YOVAN *staggers out.* MRS. BRUCHINSKI *appears with a rolling pin in her hand.*)

MRS. BRUCHINSKI. Hanky and panky, yes. Rape, no.

YOVAN. Sorry, Black Polish person. I was looking for Chris.

MRS. BRUCHINSKI. You too. Chris already busy with one lover.

YOVAN. Ah, what is the heck. I kill him later. I don't want to frighten innocent girl.

MRS. BRUCHINSKI. What girl?

YOVAN. Kris' girl lover.

MRS. BRUCHINSKI. Kris' girl lover is old man.

YOVAN. What are you saying to my ears?

MRS. BRUCHINSKI. To your ears I am saying this: Chris is into old men.

YOVAN. He has homosexual persuasions!

MRS. BRUCHINSKI. Not the Kris I thought I knew. Kris I thought I knew was not homosexual. Kris I now know is homosexual.

YOVAN. Which is the Kris I know?

MRS. BRUCHINSKI. I don't know.

YOVAN. Which Kris is in there?

MRS. BRUCHINSKI. The Kris I now know. He is into old men like gang-busters.

YOVAN. Alright, you sonuvabitch, Kris — come out with your pants up.

(CHRIS *hears this and stops typing. He jumps toward* ROGER.)

CHRIS. ROGER! ROGER! I got to go. Cover for me, all right. It's eh, eh . . . It's the F.B.I.

ROGER. The F.B.I. We're right back in the thick of things.

(CHRIS *rushes for the window. Struggles with it.* YOVAN *goes for* CHRIS' *door. He seems hestiant.* HE *knocks. Shouts.*)

YOVAN. PULL UP TROUSERS AND DROP YOUR ACTIVITY!

(CHRIS *manages to open the window.* MRS. BRUCHINSKI *goes back to her place.* YOVAN *bursts in and slams the door shut.* CHRIS *has just made it out of the window and the window drops as the door slams.* ROGER *stands confronting* YOVAN.)

So, man of no shame, this is what you are now.

ROGER. My name is Chris.

YOVAN. I know your name is Kris. I am no fool. You are into old man disguise. That does not pull wool over my eyeballs. Where is your lover boy?

ROGER. Just drop the accent, man. I know who you are.

(YOVAN *grabs him.*)

YOVAN. You're not the Kris I know! (*He pulls out gun*) Where is Kris I want to kill?

(ROGER *sees the gun and does not feel very radical.*)

ROGER. I'm not Chris you want to kill!

YOVAN. Where is other Kris?

ROGER. He left, but he'll be back. You can kill him then.

(YOVAN *lets him go.*)

YOVAN. Oh, I get it. You are old man homosexual loverboy of Kris I want to kill.

ROGER. What? Homosexual?

YOVAN. I call spade a spade. I shoot from hip.

ROGER. Wait a minute. Why do you want to kill Chris?

YOVAN. I have private snit to pick with him.

ROGER. A snit. Chris is into snits.

YOVAN. Into snits and into homosexuals like gangbusters.

ROGER. Oh, Christ, Chris! The women's movement chalks up another casualty! Oh, Chris!

(ROGER *cries bitter tears.* YOVAN *is a man moved by any tears.*)

YOVAN. Don't cry, old man, Kris.

ROGER. My name's not Chris.

YOVAN. I am glad to hear. One less Kris to worry about. Who are you, old man?

ROGER. My name is Roger.

YOVAN. Don't cry old man Roger. So you are homosexual. Big dill! I don't tell anyone.

ROGER. I'm not homosexual. I'm . . . uh . . . uh . . . Chris' father. (*He cries*)

YOVAN. Ah, now everything falls apart into place. You did not know Kris was homosexual.

ROGER. No, I did not.

YOVAN. I am sorry Papa Roger to be one to bring such news to you. (*He begins crying a little himself*) It is tough cookie to be father these days. Our children break our hearts. I never have son, but your name bring to mind the son-in-law I do have but have never laid eyes on. His name Roger too. My wife . . . she died.

ROGER. My wife . . . she left me. The slut.

YOVAN. My daughter left me and some say she slut too. Your son homosexual. My daughter slut. Our wives gone. Life is not a picnic in the park.

(*He cries bitter tears himself. He embraces* ROGER *trying to comfort him. Both weep and pat one another on the back.* MRS. BRUCHINSKI *enters. Sees two men hugging and weeping and* SHE *too starts weeping.*)

MRS. BRUCHINSKI. Men have all the fun.

YOVAN. It is no fun we are having. It is bitter tears we are shedding over children. One is gay for sure. One is slut for maybe.

MRS. BRUCHINSKI. And one is lost for good. Where is my baby boy? (*She cries too. Joins the crowd*)

YOVAN. This is not American dream come true. I am ready to throw in towel, face cloth and bath mat to boot. Too much tears in America. America used to be plenty laughs. No more. America was land of plenty. Now it's plenty of nothing and nothing is not plenty for me. Two score and one year ago I come to this country. And now what is the score? I am old. I am sad. There is pollution. There is inflation. There is no solution. I warn you, America. I go back to the old country and not think twice about looking back. I quit!! (*He suddenly smiles and cheers up*) Ah, now I feel much better. I spit bullshit poison out of my system. America, Yovan never gives up on you!

ROGER. I don't know who the hell you are but you're a helluva guy, guy.

YOVAN. That is true. When it is helluva time country needs helluva guy. I am such a man. I go now to kiss Dianah good morning. Tell Chris I kill him later on. Maybe sooner. I don't know. (*He exits*)

MRS. BRUCHINSKI. We are alone at last, old man poopsy. I don't care you are homosexual. Maybe you try go both ways, no? Acey-deucey?

ROGER. I'm not homosexual . . . although I can see where the road I'm on can lead.

MRS. BRUCHINSKI. You are not homosexual!

ROGER. Not yet.

MRS. BRUCHINSKI. Then it is time to strike while iron is hot. Let us have hanky and panky.

ROGER. Not so fast. I have to know. Are you now or have you ever been a member of the women's movement.

MRS. BRUCHINSKI. Only two movements I have been. We shall overcome movement and Polish Power movement.

ROGER. You are Polish?

MRS. BRUCHINSKI. I was adopted as young baby by Mr. and Mrs. Bruchinski. She give me her name and teach me to speak English.

ROGER. You know what you are? •

MRS. BRUCHINSKI. Vat?

ROGER. You're a quadruple minority, sister. You're a woman, you're old, Black and Polish.

MRS. BRUCHINSKI. You betchya.

ROGER. One last question. Do you know what an orgasm is?

MRS. BRUCHINSKI. Never heard of it.

ROGER. YOU'RE THE WOMAN FOR ME, MRS. B.!

(*They embrace.*)

MRS. BRUCHINSKI. Wait! We don't want unwanted babies. I have to get my diagram. (MRS. BRUCHINSKI *exits to primp and get ready*)

ROGER. She makes me feel like a macho again. Poor Chris, a macho no more.

(CHRIS *appears at the window again. He tries to open the window. Can't. He knocks on window,* ROGER *sees him. Rushes to open it. Both of them struggle. The window opens.* CHRIS *comes in.* ROGER *backs off.* CHRIS *looks very gay to him suddenly.*)

CHRIS. What's the matter with you?

ROGER. It's all right, Chris. I'm O.K. You're O.K., okay?

CHRIS. You're wrong there. I'm not O.K. at all.

ROGER. Yes, you are. You may be what you are . . . but that's okay. In my book you're still who you were.

CHRIS. No, I'm not. People change, Rog.

ROGER. I know.

CHRIS. I've changed. You've changed.

ROGER. I . . . I haven't changed like you've changed.

(ROGER *backs off from* CHRIS.)

Don't get me wrong. I have changed. But I'm still the same guy.

CHRIS. You can't have it both ways, Rog.

ROGER. I don't want to have it both ways. Chris, I know the truth about you.

CHRIS. I was going to tell you myself. I guess that guy Yovan told you all about it.

ROGER. Yes. I didn't believe him. I mean I . . .

CHRIS. It's true.

ROGER. Oh, God. I better go to L.A. right away. Don't get me wrong. I still love you. LIKE A BROTHER.

CHRIS. I don't know how I love you.

ROGER. I'D PREFER IT LIKE A BROTHER, Chris.

CHRIS. Like a brother it is.

ROGER. Oh, Chris. I understand. What with the way the women are, it's a wonder we're all not, you know. I don't want to hurt you, but when it comes to sex . . . I'm on the other side.

CHRIS. Oh, Rog, I didn't know.

ROGER. I didn't think you did.

CHRIS. When did it happen?

ROGER. It never happened. I was always on the other side.

CHRIS. All those years!

ROGER. Yeah, but we were all on the same side for all those years.

CHRIS. No, we weren't. I was always . . .

ROGER. You weren't really, were you, Chris? All those years.

CHRIS. Everybody was, I guess, except for you. All the guys were . . .

ROGER. All the guys! Not all the guys! Jerry, Abbie . . . Billy Kunstler?

CHRIS. Rennie Davis . . . Tom Hayden.

ROGER. TOM TOO! Stop. Stop it, Chris!

CHRIS. It's all right, Rog. There's no right or wrong in this matter. You can be gay.

(ROGER *clutches his head.*)

ROGER. No, Chris. I can't.
CHRIS. Sure you can. It's fine with me.
ROGER. I know it's fine with you!
CHRIS. What are friends for?
ROGER. Not for that!

(HE *backs away from* CHRIS. CHRIS *is puzzled.*)

CHRIS. You're acting real queer, Rog.
ROGER. No, I'm not. I am not either. I can't, Chris. I can't. I'm not gay. I don't want to be gay. Please. You can be gay, but you can't be gay with me.
CHRIS. What are you talking about? I'm not gay.
ROGER. You're not? But that F.B.I. guy . . . (*He slaps his head*) I fell for it! It was all a cheap F.B.I. trick!
CHRIS. Oh, no. He's not F.B.I.
ROGER. Then he's C.I.A. Crooked bastards tried to make us think we're not straight. We're real guys. Both of us. I love you once again, Chris!

(*He flies into* CHRIS' *arms and starts kissing him on the cheek.* MRS. BRUCHINSKI *walks in and sees the two men hugging. She makes a big gesture of despair and starts to leave.* ROGER *sees her.*)

Mrs. Bruchinski, Chris is not gay.
MRS. BRUCHINSKI. And you?
ROGER. Me neither!
MRS. BRUCHINSKI. Praise Jesus! A miracle! Now I am ready to sin like gangbusters.
ROGER. MRS. BRU, I'M READY FOR YOU!
MRS. BRUCHINSKI. I'm time for hanky and panky!

(*She grabs* ROGER *and pulls him into* CHRIS' *bedroom. They shut the door behind them.* CHRIS *just stands*

there, ossified. He takes his typewriter and paper.
Goes to his bedroom door.)

CHRIS. Since you're using my apartment, Mrs.
Bruchinski, I'm going to use yours. Okay?
ROGER/MRS. BRUCHINSKI. OKAY!

(NADJA *appears in the street and is heading toward*
CHRIS' *building as* CHRIS *is heading out of his*
apartment into MRS. BRUCHINSKI'S *apartment.*
NADJA *comes up the stairs just as* CHRIS *shuts the*
door. NADJA *enters* CHRIS' *apartment. She has a*
package with her. It's some different clothes she
has brought.)

NADJA. Chris?

(*She's almost glad he's there. She smiles and goes*
into the bathroom with her package to change. As
she shuts the door on the bathroom YOVAN *appears*
at the window. He is holding a tear gas cannister in
his hand.)

YOVAN. Allo you in there! This is me out here! This is
to make plenty sure you understand I mean beez-wax!

(*He throws the grenade inside and vanishes. Smoke*
starts coming out of the grenade. The door to
CHRIS' *bedroom bursts open.* ROGER *stands there*
without his trousers, the rest of his makeup intact.
He sniffs the air.)

ROGER. IT'S TEAR GAS! OH, MY GOD, IT'S
REALLY TEAR GAS! I LOVE IT! I LOVE IT! (*He*
sniffs the air like a man afflicted with rampaging

nostalgia. He picks up the grenade and runs to the window. He throws it out. Fists wave in the air) Jerry, Abbie, Rennie, we're back in business! The whole world is watching! The whole world is watching!

(*The door to the bathroom opens.* NADJA *comes out in a different outfit.* ROGER *is at the window.*)

NADJA. What happened in here?

(ROGER *turns around and lets out a scream.*)

ROGER. NADJA!
NADJA. Oh, Chris told you about me.
ROGER. NADJA!
NADJA. Is something the matter with you?
ROGER. IT'S ME! YOU DID THIS TO ME, YOU!

(*He comes toward her.* NADJA *screams.* ROGER *pursues her.* MRS. BRUCHINSKI *comes out.* ROGER *is screaming.* NADJA *is screaming.* MRS. BRUCHINSKI *is looking on. At an opportune moment, she slugs* ROGER. ROGER *goes out like a candle.*)

MRS. BRUCHINSKI. He is helluva old man. But he's mine. Okay?
NADJA. Sure. Take him. Where is Chris?
MRS. BRUCHINSKI. Chris is out. You are whore in different clothes, no?
NADJA. No, I'm not going to be a whore anymore.
MRS. BRUCHINSKI. Praise Jesus! Miracle number two! It is a day of conversion!
NADJA. I have to go find my father and tell him the happy news.

(YOVAN *appears on the street, coughing from the tear gas.*)

Tell Chris I'll be back.

(NADJA *and* MRS. BRUCHINSKI *go out.* NADJA *goes down the stairs and out into the street and Off.* YOVAN *coughing does not see her.* MRS. BRUCHINSKI *goes into her apartment. And then* CHRIS *comes out of her apartment with his typewriter. Goes into his apartment.* YOVAN *is coming up the stairs.* CHRIS *is looking at* ROGER *on the floor.* YOVAN *comes up to the landing.* MRS. BRUCHINSKI *flings open her door. Catches* YOVAN *in the face. Marches right on. Opens* CHRIS' *door. Goes in as* YOVAN *is recovering a little.*)

MRS. BRUCHINSKI. Chris. I forgot to tell you. She will be back.
CHRIS. Who will be back?
MRS. BRUCHINSKI. Whore who is whore no more.

(*She swings the door open as she goes out. Catches* YOVAN *on the face again, leaving* CHRIS' *door open and goes into her place.* CHRIS *sees the open door. Goes to close it.* YOVAN *shook up by the blow falls against the door, slamming it shut. As the door shuts the window falls down.* CHRIS *looks at one and the then the other. He sniffs the air.*)

CHRIS. I must be losing my mind. Sure, I'm losing my mind. I'm talking to myself and I smell tear gas.

(ROGER *is recovering from his blow. He is getting up slowly.*)

ROGER. Where is she?

CHRIS. Where is who?

(ROGER *sees* CHRIS.)

ROGER. Chris. My wife was here!

CHRIS. Oh, Rog. Please. She wasn't here. I was the only guy who was here and even I wasn't here. I was next door.

ROGER. She hurled a cannister of tear gas in here.

CHRIS. You smell it too? Your mind is gone, Rog. And mine is going. So, I'm going too. (*He starts to leave*)

ROGER. Where are you going?

CHRIS. If I'm going to go out of my mind, I'd just as soon go out in the street and go out of it there. We're both out of it, anyway. We're out of it, man. I'm leaving. Bye-bye.

(CHRIS *opens the door just as* YOVAN *has recovered and is standing up ready to come at him.* YOVAN *screams.* CHRIS *runs back into room and shuts the door, but not fully.*)

It's the C.I.A. guy. He wants to kill me.

(*He can't shut the door fully because* YOVAN *is pulling on it.*)

ROGER. Then we'll both die. We'll die together.

YOVAN. Open door somonabitch. (YOVAN *fires gun at door. He finally triumphs over* CHRIS. *He opens the door, bursts in. Shuts the door behind him. Fires gun again*) Okee-dokey! Now we get down to beez-wax!

(CHRIS *is thinking visibly.*)

CHRIS. Ah, listen. Ah . . . my . . . My father here is very sick.

(ROGER *doesn't know what he's getting at, but he's trying. There's a plan in the air.*)

A bad heart! If you kill me the shock would kill him too!

(ROGER *gets it.*)

ROGER. He's my only boy. Shoot if you must these gray hairs but spare my boy.
YOVAN. Oh! To find such love between Papa and son in these times is a subject worthy of small talk.

(ROGER *is hugging and kissing* CHRIS.)

ROGER. He's an angel. The apple of my eye!
YOVAN. He is also the grape of my wrath! But what is the heck. Redical son make apple-ogy and I give full pardon and amnesty.
ROGER. Pardon. Amnesty. Apologize! Never! We are radicals and we will die radicals. Shoot us. We don't mind dying. I'd just as soon die as go to Los Angeles anyway. Shoot us!
CHRIS. Shut up, Roger!

(YOVAN *threatens* CHRIS.)

YOVAN. YOU! Not to talk to old father in such way. In old country Papa gets respect.
ROGER. Blow it out your ear, you C.I.A. stooge. Your old country sucks!

(YOVAN *is mortified. He is ready to turn his wrath on*
    ROGER. CHRIS *realizes things are going badly.*)

CHRIS. Shut your damned mouth, Roger!

(YOVAN'S *wrath switches.*)

YOVAN. YOU! Not to call Papa by first name basis.
Papa is Papa. (*He pushes* CHRIS *into sofa. Confronts*
ROGER) Okee-dokey, old Papa. Maybe now you tell me
which old country makes suck!
    ROGER. Which old country are you from?
    YOVAN. In no tell you. So there. HA! HA!

(HE *laughs.* ROGER *is furious.*)

ROGER. Poland! Poland sucks.
YOVAN. Poland is no skin off my nose.
ROGER. Czechoslovakia!
YOVAN. Hmmm.
ROGER. Lithuania!
YOVAN. Ha, ha, ha.
ROGER. Estonia! Bulgaria! Rumania! Albania!
YOVAN. You are right. Albania, it is true, sucks.
ROGER. Greece sucks!
YOVAN. You are right.
ROGER. Cyprus, Italy, Spain. They all suck. Turkey
sucks!
YOVAN. Do you think Turkey sucks?
ROGER. Yes, Turkey sucks.
YOVAN. I wasn't sure. I think you are right. Turkey
sucks.

(ROGER *is just about foaming at the mouth.*)

ROGER. That's it! There are no more old countries!

YOVAN. You forget Yugoslavia!

ROGER. YUGOSLAVIA IS THE SUCK CHAMP OF EUROPE!

YOVAN. NOW I KILL YOU! You make apple-ogy or I make you dead.

ROGER. Never!

CHRIS. Make apple-ogy, Roger.

YOVAN. NOT TO CALL PAPA, ROGER! YOU LET PAPA DIE IN RESPECT!

(*He cocks his pistol and points it at* ROGER.)

Now, either I hear apple-ogy or by gosh I shoot you down like son's car.

ROGER. You dumb Yugoslavian. My son doesn't have a car.

YOVAN. You stupid American. Maybe you ask somonabitch son about his car!

(ROGER *is mildly suspicious. Both turn eyes toward* CHRIS.)

ROGER. Tell him, son. Tell him you don't have a car.

CHRIS. I, well, I had a car, Papa.

ROGER. O—o-o-h!

YOVAN. O—o-o-h!

CHRIS. O—o-o-h!

YOVAN. How come Papa not know. Son never give Papa ride in car down Michigan Avenue.

ROGER. No, never. Maybe son take Papa on different kind of ride. Maybe my boy is not such a good boy after all.

YOVAN. Not to jump to conclusion! Maybe son so upset about divorce he forget.

ROGER. Divorce! My son had a divorce?

YOVAN. You did not know?

ROGER. I did not know son was married.

(*Both of them look at* CHRIS.)

CHRIS. Papa never asked.

YOVAN. Papa not have to ask! What kind cold cut baloney is that. (*To* ROGER) Kids today. My daughter. She is the same way. She stab me in the heart.

ROGER. Yes, but my son stabbed me in the back. He's a bad boy, my son.

(ROGER *slaps* CHRIS' *face.*)

YOVAN. I told you so.

CHRIS. Damn you, Roger! You never gave me a chance. You started raving like a lunatic about your slutty wife . . .

YOVAN. YOU CALL PAPA'S WIFE SLUTTY!

CHRIS. He called her a slut himself.

ROGER. He has no respect.

YOVAN. Papa can call wife slut. Son cannot call mother slut!

CHRIS. His wife is not my mother.

YOVAN. Same applies to step-mother.

CHRIS. Oh, the hell with it. You see, he's not my father.

ROGER. You see. He has no respect.

YOVAN. He's a rotten brat, that much is true. To spill lunch, in my place and then say it is the poisoning of the food!

ROGER. Poisoning of the food!

YOVAN. Yes, stuffed cabbage.

ROGER. Days of Vomit was a stuffed cabbage, Chris! ALL THIS WAS A STUFFED CABBAGE! CHRIS . . . Spartacus . . . you . . . you too.

CHRIS. Me too, Rog. I've done it all, from A to Z, but if you want I'll begin in the middle with M for Movement.

(ROGER *is near tears.*)

ROGER. Oh, no, Chris.
CHRIS. Oh, yes, Rog.
ROGER. The movement?
CHRIS. All gone.

(ROGER *is in tears.* YOVAN *can't understand what has happened.* ROGER *is weeping.*)

ROGER. Our youth.
CHRIS. All gone too.
ROGER. Oh. Chris. (ROGER *goes to him. Embraces him*) Oh, world. Oh, life.
CHRIS. Oh, Rog.
YOVAN. Oh, my gosh.

(ROGER *suddenly knows what he has to do.*)

ROGER. That's it! I don't want to live without hope. Let's die. A double suicide, Chris. Give me the gun. I'll kill myself.

(*He runs at* YOVAN. *He wants the gun to shoot himself.* CHRIS *tries to stop him.* YOVAN *even tries to stop him. There's a possibility here of a gun going off. The door opens and in walks* DIANAH *with the bullhorn. The fighting continues as she looks on. She puts the bullhorn to her lips.*)

DIANAH. WHAT THE HELL IS GOING ON?

(*The struggle ceases. All eyes turn toward her. She shuts the door.* YOVAN *is glad to see her. She is shocked to see him.* CHRIS *is annoyed to see her but glad for the intrusion.* ROGER *is nothing yet. He heads for the window.*)

YOVAN. Dianah!

DIANAH. Yovan!

CHRIS. Dianah!

DIANAH. Chris. (*To* YOVAN) I didn't know you knew Chris.

YOVAN. I knew you knew a Chris but I did not know that the Chris I know is the Chris you know.

DIANAH. It is. I didn't know you knew Yovan, Chris.

CHRIS. I didn't know you knew Yovan either, Dianah.

YOVAN. We all know each other but I don't know how we all know so much!

(DIANAH *goes to* CHRIS.)

DIANAH. Oh, what does it matter. You say tomato, and he says tomahto. You say potato and he says potahto. Potato, potahto, tomato, tomahto . . . Chris, let's call the whole thing off.

CHRIS. Has something happened to you that I should know about?

DIANAH. I'm in love with somebody else.

YOVAN. Who?

DIANAH. You.

YOVAN. Good.

DIANAH. He makes me feel like a woman and I feel like feeling like a woman. I'm sorry, Chris. It was just one of those things, just one of those fabulous flings. A

trip to the moon on gossamer wings. But I can't be your
wife anymore.

YOVAN. WIFE!

CHRIS. Wonderful.

YOVAN. Not so wonderful so quickly. I did not know
you were married.

DIANAH. I was, I am. But I won't be for long.

YOVAN. Ach, somonabitch. I did not know that the
woman I find and the wife you lose is same woman.
Gosh, dammit. This takes the cup cake. I come here to
offer pardon to Chris and now I have to ask Chris for
pardon. Chris, sorry.

CHRIS. Ah, what is the heck.

(*They embrace.* NADJA *appears in the street. She heads
for* CHRIS' *apartment building.*)

DIANAH. I love this. My past and my future stand
before me embracing in the windy city where it all
began. I even smell tear gas . . .

ROGER. I smell a rat. I'm going to pack up and leave.

(*He goes into the bedroom and shuts the door. The
front door opens and in walks* NADJA. *All eyes are
on her.*)

CHRIS. Roger! Nadja!

NADJA. Chris!

YOVAN. Nadja!

NADJA. Daddy!

CHRIS. DADDY!

DIANAH. Daddy!

YOVAN. Nadja my little girl. Oh, I love you like the
son I never had. But what the holy heck are you doing
here?

NADJA. I'm doing political work with Chris, Daddy.

YOVAN. I didn't know you knew Chris.

NADJA. I didn't know you knew Chris either. (*To* CHRIS) I didn't know you knew my father.

DIANAH. I didn't know you had a daughter.

YOVAN. I didn't know you had a husband.

NADJA. I love Chris, Daddy.

YOVAN. You love Chris, but you're married.

NADJA. I'm divorced, Daddy.

YOVAN. And where is your husband Roger?

CHRIS. Husband Roger! Oh, no!

(ROGER *appears with his belongings at the bedroom door. HE sees* NADJA.)

ROGER. Revenge! I smell Revenge!

NADJA. I'm glad you're up and at it, Gramps.

ROGER. I'm not up, Nadja.

NADJA. You look up to me.

ROGER. There she goes again. Orgasms, orgasms!

NADJA. He sounds like my husband, Roger.

ROGER. I am your husband Roger.

(*He briefly lifts off his wig, then quickly replaces it.* YOVAN *gasps.*)

NADJA. Daddy, I'd like you to meet my ex-husband and your ex-son-in-law, Roger.

YOVAN. By gosh, this takes the cup cake, too. So you are son-in-law Roger! The less names there are the more confusing the people who are left behind.

(*All start trying to explain.*)

STOP! EVERYBODY MAKE HUSH!

(*Silence.*)

I have to figure out stuff. (HE *begins putting it all together. Points to* NADJA) You are my daughter. I begin with easy stuff first. And you were married to my ex-son-in-law who is the father of the ex-husband of my wife to be. (*Points to* CHRIS) You are Chris. Your Papa ran off with my daughter. (*Points at* ROGER) You are Roger. Your son Chris, no your step-son, Chris, is the step-son also of my daughter Nadja, your ex-wife. (*Points to* CHRIS *again*) Therefore, you Chris are my step-grandson. No, since my daughter Nadja divorced your Papa, you are my ex-step-grandson and your ex-wife, your Papa's daughter-in-law, will be my daughter's stepmother. Yeah. Now it's all clear. Bravo! At last I have big family. (*He starts hugging one and all*)

ROGER. What about me? Am I to be left to turn slowly in the wind. What about the movement, Chris?

CHRIS. I told you, Rog. It's over.

(MRS. BRUCHINSKI *enters.*)

ROGER. No, there's still Mrs. Bruchinski. We are the movement now. It's you and me, Mrs. B.

MRS. BRUCHINSKI. We march to Washington.

(*A whistle blows.* BETTY *and* SAL *burst in.*)

BETTY. Everybody freeze! Police! (*Sees* CHRIS) Chris.

CHRIS. J.B.
BETTY. Nadja.
NADJA. Betty.
DIANAH. Sal!
SAL. Dianah.

YOVAN. Here we go one more time again, I betcha!

SAL. Oh, my God. So many people. And I know some of them. It's my first reunion.

ROGER. J.B.! I thought I recognized you.

BETTY. And who're you, Gramps?!

ROGER. It's me! Roger. Roger O'Dwyer.

BETTY. Roger!

ROGER. J.B.!

(*They do their old time greeting handshake.*)

NADJA. I didn't know you knew Chris and Roger, Betty.

BETTY. I didn't know you knew them either.

NADJA. I was married to one and I love the other.

BETTY. Which is which?

(*All try to answer at once.*)

YOVAN. STOP! PLEASE! I AM GETTING A PAIN IN MY HEADACHE! I already explain which is which and who is who and why is for. I beg you on folded legs let us not do it again, Miss!

ROGER. She's not really a Miss. She's a he.

BETTY. The name's Officer Kellogg.

SAL. My last name is Kellogg.

BETTY. Your last name is Kellogg?

MRS. BRUCHINSKI. I had a cute baby boy with an old man Kellogg.

SAL & BETTY. I was a cute baby boy named Kellogg.

MRS. BRUCHINSKI. But old man Kellogg . . . he lost my baby boy on Division Street.

BETTY. I WAS FOUND ON DIVISION STREET!

MRS. BRUCHINSKI. YOU ARE FOUND ONCE AGAIN! MY BOY!

BETTY. MAMA!

(*They embrace.*)

SAL. Close, but no cigar.

MRS. BRUCHINSKI. You also have brother somewhere. Old man Kellogg told me he left his first son with a baby sitter.

SAL. I was left with a baby sitter!

MRS. BRUCHINSKI. All paid for?

SAL. All paid for!

MRS. BRUCHINSKI. Then you have a father in common.

SAL. Sister!

BETTY. Brother!

(SAL *and* BETTY *embrace.*)

SAL. It was incest! But I didn't know.

(MRS. BRUCHINSKI *embraces both of them.*)

MRS. BRUCHINSKI. My kids!

SAL & BETTY. MAMA!

(*She cries tears of joy.* YOVAN *is moved too.*)

YOVAN. ONLY IN AMERICA! Black and white and Polish and Jewish and they kiss and hug like gangbusters. Where else do you find such stuff but in America? I was born in the old country, but my dreams were born in America. The dream . . . it lives!

MRS. BRUCHINSKI. We shall overcome, you crazy man!

YOVAN. Yes, Black Polish person, we shall overcome like gangbusters.

SAL. I am overcome already.

DIANAH. Oh, it brings back the old days to hear you speak like that.

ROGER. Chris! Can you feel it. It's happening again. We're not alone.

CHRIS. C'mon, Rog. It's over.

ROGER. The long night is over. The new dawn of history is at hand. Look . . . look around . . . what do you see?

BETTY. The movement Chris. It moves again.

DIANAH. It does. I can feel it.

(ROGER *is getting all choked up with emotion.*)

ROGER. It's all here! THE NEW COALITION! IT'S THE NEW COALITION!

ALL. WE'RE THE NEW COALITION!

BETTY. Right on, Rog!

SAL. Right on Rog.

MRS. BRUCHINSKI. Bravo for you old man, poopsy!

ROGER. Look. Look around. Men! Women! Black! White! Polish! Jewish! Protestant! Catholic!

DIANAH. Agnostic!

YOVAN. Serbian Orthodox!

BETTY. Transsexual!

NADJA. Neosexual!

MRS. BRUCHINSKI. Over sexual!

SAL. Under sexual!

ROGER. The lost tribe of the American Dream.

ALL. Yea!

ROGER. It's the new beginning. The new coalition. The new movement!

YOVAN. THE NEW WORLD BAR AND GRILL!

ROGER. Chris. Lead us. Lead us again.

CHRIS. I just want to lead my life and that's all.

DIANAH. Here, Chris. Take the old bullhorn and play it again. Play it again, Chris.

CHRIS. No more playing. I'm tired of playing.

YOVAN. Son, take the bull by horn and speak.

CHRIS. What do you want from me. Nobody gives a damn anymore.

ROGER. I still give a damn.

CHRIS. You're crazy. That's why.

DIANAH. You were crazy once yourself!

ROGER. You were a magnificent crazy sonovabitch!

CHRIS. Oh yeah, and where did it get me.

YOVAN. It got you to Chicago . . . To Division Street . . . to me . . . YOVAN . . . I have mimeo machine. We make leaflets.

DIANAH. And the smell of mimeo ink will be heard throughout the land again.

SAL. The little guy is ready to march.

BETTY. The women's movement throws in its support to the New Movement.

NADJA. The unemployed youth vote is yours, Chris.

MRS. BRUCHINSKI. I give you Black Polish support.

ROGER. We've got them all, baby.

BETTY. Including the cross-over vote!

CHRIS. I don't believe this. I don't believe any of this.

ROGER. But wasn't it nice when we believed in it all. America, Chris. Remember.

YOVAN. America! AMERICA. I love it.

CHRIS. You think I don't . . . You're all crazy . . .

(*They all begin to talk.*)

Look . . . listen to me . . . There were thousands. There were thousands upon thousands . . . there were millions and now . . . look . . . there . . . There's eight of us. What are we going to do with eight people.

ROGER. Look what they did with seven in "The Magnificent Seven." I see the spark, Chris. I see it in your eye. Don't let it die.

CHRIS. Listen to me. I've done my part. I've warned you. I've told you it's hopeless and that you haven't got a chance. I tried it once and it didn't work. But, I guess there's always a second time. Be a shame to let the new coalition go to waste. Without me you're just the Chicago Seven all over again. So let's do it.

ROGER. What?

CHRIS. Let's do it and do it right this time.

(*All cheer.*)

There's eight of us. We're eight for the eighties!

(*Cheers.*)

I've stood by long enough. I think it's time to move again. I don't know where that road is I saw so clearly when I was young, but I know it's there, and I know we can find it if we try. (*He grabs the bullhorn and leaps onto the sofa*) So let's try.

(*Cheers.*)

It's not going to be easy. At every step they will tell us that we've had our chance and failed. The voice of despair will tell us that we have had it. And we will re- ply: YES. We have had it. We've had it with the Republicans and we've had it with the Democrats. We've had it with the right wing and we've had it with the left wing.

(*Cheers, yells, applause.*)

This is our manifesto. When the leaders, whoever they are, do not inspire, then we will not follow. When the leaders, whoever they are, try to divide us, we will press all the closer together.

(ROGER *joins in on this one.*)

When the world we envision is better than the one we live in, we will follow our vision. And when they tell us, that the frontier is gone we will reply: The frontiers of dreamers is endless and we still have a dream.

(YOVAN *begins singing "America the Beautiful" and others join in.* CHRIS' *voice rises above their singing.*)

It is a time of transition and in those times false prophets and false fears spread throughout the land, but new spirits also arise. New dreams are born and a glorious struggle takes place for the soul of the nation. The struggle is on. Let it be said it began right here on Division Street. CITIZENS OF THE UNITED STATES OF AMERICA . . .

(*The group breaks into the chorus of "America."*)

It is a new decade and I proclaim in the name of the new decade, the birth of a new movement, the second movement of the great American symphony. The ring of freedom is our tuning fork, hope is our music, America is our song!

(*The group surrounds* CHRIS. *Suddenly we hear "America the Beautiful" sung by a huge choir. The company hears it and joins in, marching into the streets.*)

Cʜᴏɪʀ & Cᴏᴍᴘᴀɴʏ (*Singing.*)

O beautiful for spacious skies, for amber waves of grain
For purple mountain majesties, above the fruited plain!
America! America! God shed His grace on thee,
And crown thy good with brotherhood, from sea to
    shining sea.

O beautiful for pilgrim feet whose stern impassioned
    stress
O thoroughfare for freedom beat, across the wilderness!
America! America! God mend thine every flaw,
Confirm thy soul in self-control, by liberty in law.

O beautiful for patriot dream, that sees beyond the
    years
Thine alabaster cities gleam, undimmed by human
    tears!
America! America! God shed His grace on thee,
And crown thy good with brotherhood, from sea to
    shining sea.

CURTAIN

PROPERTY LIST

SET Interior
Stove
Pots (3)
Coffee pot
Frying Pan
Sink
Assorted Dishes in sink
Sponges (2)
Assorted Kitchen supplies
Curtain below sink
Refrigerator
Cartons of milk (numerous)
Wooden Crates (5)
Food supplies
Waste Basket
Mop
Bucket
Lunch box
Wooden picture frames (2)
Assorted books & magazines
Blue bed spread
Old quilts (2)
Radiator
Dresser
Cardboard boxes (2)
Radio
Alarm Clock
Assorted Clothes
Accordian File Folder
Old speeches

Assorted manila envelopes &
  folders
Shoebox
Wall mirror
Ties (2)
Guitar Case
Ladder
Paint cans (3)
Paint buckets (3)
Roller brush
Paint brush
Large Quilt
Mattress
Small Trunk
Small Wooden Box
Assorted books & magazines
Large pillows (2)
Couch
Assorted socks, etc.
  underneath couch
Quilt on couch
Brown pants
Yellow shirt
Green bedspread
Small pillows (2)
Ottoman
Large Trunk
Dial phone w/cord
Plates (2)
Knife

Fork
Mugs (2)
Cup
Glass
Book
Alka Selzer bottles (2)
Mints (several)
Fly swatter
Sun-Times
Red glass
Large Oriental Rug
Medium Oriental Rugs
   (5 x 7)
Small Oriental Rugs (3 x 5)
Chandeliers (2)
Wall sconce

BATHROOM
Shower curtain (2)
Towel rack
Bath towels (3)
Hand towel
Wash cloth
Throw rug

BEDROOM
End table
Lamp
Assorted books
Sticks of wood (2)

MRS. B's
Fan
Dish Towel
Plate
Mug
Rolling Pin
Small table

Figurines (5)
Picture frame
Small rug (2 x 3)
Lace cloth
Pictures (3)
Black jewelry box w/mirror
Wooden decorative palm
   tree
Trash can lid
Cymbol

SET Exterior
UR
   Large trash cans—full (3)
   Large garbage bags—full
      (2)
   Green cushion
   Chaise lounge cushion
   Wooden crates (2)
Milk Carrier w/milk cartons
Benches (2)
Pay phone
Street lamps (2)
Traffic signs (7)
Assorted flier and
   announcements
American flag

UL
   Large trash cans—full (4)
   Large garbage bags—full
      (2)
   Green cushion
   Wooden crates (2)
   Board
   Paint buckets (2)

HAND PROPS

Poloroid pronto
Black briefcase
Foil wrapped cabbage
Smith & Wesson Special
38 calibre 5" barrel
Tear gas cannister
Dime
Foreign papers (11)
Sun-Times (10)
Tribune (7)
Bomb (28")
Restaurant card
Shaver
Whistle
Sam Brown belt
Billy club
Colt 38 calibre 5" barrel
NY Times
Bullhorn
Grey attache case
Black attache case
Marshall Fields dress box
Red appointment book
Spray perfume bottle
Car top
Large handled brown paper
  bag
Small handled brown paper
  bag

Plastic handled bag
Assorted clothes for stuffing
Sleeping bag
Canvass bag
Cassette recorder/FM radio
Cassette of "Those Were
  The Days"
Pill bottle
Sweet & Sour Smarties
Social Security card
Paper with address
Typewriter
Cup & Saucer
Rat poisen can
Blank typing paper (2)
Half typed letter (1)
Full typed letter (2)
Pencil
Crumpled up paper (3)

Offstage
Colt snub nosed 38 calibre
Full load blanks
Gun for firing papers
Tribunes (3)

COSTUME PLOT

Chris

Act I Rumpled three piece suit
Rumpled white shirt with brown & red window-
pane check
Brown belt
Brown hush puppy's
Wire rim glasses
2nd entrance Change to brown tweed jacket
Act II Light brown corduroy jeans
Light blue work shirt
Brown belt
Sneakers

Yovan

Act I Black double-breasted suit with maroon pin
& stripe
Act II Black patent leather wing tips with pointed toes
Maroon nylon socks
Black felt hat
Several large, garish rings
He wears all of the above throughout the show
but changes into a different shirt and tie for
each entrance. All of them are very LOUD:
paisley, stripes, patterns. Also he wears a different buttoniere for each entrance.

Sal

Act I Gray suit
Blue & white stripe shirt
Grey socks

Grey shoes
Grey & blue stripe tie
Grey brief case
(All the greys should be the same shade)

Act II Grey oversize nylon raincoat
Grey tank type undershirt
Grey pattern boxer shorts
Same socks & shoes
Grey sock garters

2nd entrance 1st Act pants, shoes, socks
Large grey sweatshirt with POLICE ATHLET-
IC LEAGUE in blue letters on the front
and BETTY on the back.
Blue policeman's cap

Roger

Act I Ratty brown wool overcoat, very large
& Ratty torn, stained brown cords
Act II Old black high top sneakers
Ratty torn brown vest
Old rust pattern tie
Faded, rumpled orangish pattern shirt
White, green, orange pattern boxer shorts
Old, matted, dirty white wig
Orange T-shirt with large peace sign stenciled
on it in white
Battered brown felt hat
Brown fingerless gloves
He is in and out of these pieces throughout the
show, but doesn't show the T-shirt until the
end.

Betty

Act I Blue police womans uniform — jacket, skirt,
& blouse
Act II Blue pumps

Stockings
Blue police womans cap
Girdle with hip padding
* Very padded bra
Slip
Black wig
Whistle attached to jacket

Mrs. Bruchinski

Act I Pink flowered zipfront robe dress
Pink scuffs
Multi-colored horizontal stripe socks rolled
    down
Colorful peasant type apron
Grey wig

Act II Long blue, green, white print cotton robe
Large multicolor peasant type shawl
Blue ruffled nylon curler cap

2nd entrance Act I dress, scuffs, socks, apron
Multi-color peasant type vest
Large pink beaded earrings
Several strands long pink bead necklace

3rd entrance Same as above
Flowers pinned in hair

Nadja

Act I Hot pink milliskin halter top with padlock
    closing
Hot pink milliskin mini skirt
Orange hot pants
Large chain belt with padlock
Large gaudy earrings
Several bright color plastic bracelets
Chain ankle bracelet with keys hanging from it
Blue/green open toe heels
Red bra & panties

          Act II Same as Act I
2nd entrance White with pink lacy dress (very pure and
                  virginal)
              White ballet slippers with pink flowers
              Pink flower headband
              Nude tone bra and panties
                  (removes all other jewelry)

Dianah
          Act I Blue jeans (designer)
                  Lilac cotton indian shirt
                  Darker lilac macrame belt
                  Purple low heeled shoes
                  Sunglasses with very dark lenses
                  Gold hoop earrings
                  Gauze purple, blue, gold indian scarf — very
                      long
          Act II Same jeans
                  Purple silk Indian shirt
                  Same belt
                  Indian earrings and necklace
                  Feathers and beads in hair
                  Same shoes